Chunky Knits

Chunky Knits

Stylish and quick designs made with super-size needles

Lauren Aston

CICO BOOKS

LONDON NEW YORK

To Ena and Jean, my lovely grandmothers, for teaching me how to knit—they'd have loved this!

This edition published in 2024 by CICO Books
An imprint of Ryland Peters & Small Ltd
20–21 Jockey's Fields   341 E 116th St
London WC1R 4BW   New York, NY 10029

www.rylandpeters.com

10 9 8 7 6 5 4 3 2 1

First published in 2017 as *Super Chunky Knits*

Text © Lauren Aston 2017, 2024
Design, illustration, and photography © CICO
Books 2017, 2024

A CIP catalog record for this book is available from the Library of Congress and the British Library.

ISBN: 978-1-80065-367-2

Printed in China

Editor Kate Haxell
Pattern checkers Kate Haxell and Marilyn Wilson
Designer Sarah Rock
Photographer Penny Wincer
Stylist Joanna Thornhill
Illustrator Stephen Dew

Art director Sally Powell
Production controller David Hearn
Publishing manager Penny Craig
Production manager Gordana Simakovic
Publisher Cindy Richards

FSC
www.fsc.org
MIX
Paper from responsible sources
FSC® C106563

Contents

Introduction

My grandmother taught me to knit when I was 11 years old, and I instantly loved the satisfaction I got from successfully knitting something from scratch. Another thing I soon learnt was that needles smaller than US 15 (10mm) just weren't my bag! It took a few more years of hard work and a degree in knitwear to really understand and appreciate the craft. When it came to starting my business I knew I wanted to do something creative—and ideally wanted to be knitting—but I also knew that the work needed to be quite speedy to make, and the answer to that would be using the thickest wool I could find. Giant knitting didn't really exist at the time, so it was a long search and a lot of development before I finally figured it all out and launched my brand at the beginning of 2015. I now work from my home studio in beautiful Devon, spending my days hand-knitting and pinching myself to confirm that this really is my life. I create super-chunky goodies—mainly soft furnishings as well as some knitwear and Christmas pieces.

I love the tactility of making something so big and cozy, and when CICO approached me about writing a book I realized it was time to share that with other like-minded knitters. If you've never tried super-chunky or giant knitting before, I hope this book will be a friendly introduction. A lot of the projects in it are fun and vibrant, and the beauty of this gigantic wool is that it knits up quickly—most of the designs can easily be made over a weekend, and some in a matter of hours.

With projects for both new and experienced knitters, in a range of sizes and scales, there should be something for everyone. Super-chunky and giant knitting is great for beginners because it's so easy to see where your stitches are and what you're doing with them. Experienced knitters will hopefully enjoy the challenge of knitting on the giant needles, seeing their work develop quickly and clearly, and using stitches they're no doubt familiar with but that look wonderfully different on such a large scale.

I've thoroughly enjoyed developing such a diverse selection of knits, from giant blankets, to Christmas trees, hanging plantholders, and fingerless gloves. This collection of homely and cozy makes blends traditional styles with playful pops of color and a bit of a wacky scale. Never wanting to waste such lovely yarn, there's also a number of pom-pom-based projects that are perfect for using up your last offcuts of yarn. Overall, it's a stylish yet playful collection of makes, and I hope you enjoy knitting them as much as I did creating them. Please do share your results with me on social media using #laurenastondesigns as it would be brilliant to see what you've knitted up!

Lauren Aston

CHAPTER ONE

For You

Warm and cozy accessories are perfect for transitioning through the seasons. Layer up with fun gloves, textured snoods, and pom-pom beanie hats in the winter, and enjoy tactile and comfortable headbands to keep your ears snug in the spring. This diverse collection of knits offers a playful and updated twist on traditional key pieces. The Jumbo Cuffs (see page 26) are a brilliant starting point as they are quick and easy to make—you can whip them up in every color and have a pair for any occasion, be it dinner and drinks or just walking the dog. The Striped Fingerless Gloves (see page 46) and the Twisted and Turban-style Headbands (see pages 14 and 38) are really quick knits—ideal as last-minute gifts—but my personal favorite is the Cable-knit Hand Muff (see page 36), which brings an indulgently comfy cable knit to spring walks or winter weddings.

Changing colors in very thick yarn can be a little problematic—you don't want to end up with lots of huge loose ends to sew in as this can affect the overall shape of the knit. But changing just once is very manageable, and when it's done in this scale it makes a real impact. I used dark gray and off-white for the main scarf so that you could really see the contrast—yet the monotone keeps it from being too bold—and then added a pop of color and fun with the bright pink pom-poms.

Color-block Giant-knit Scarf

SKILL LEVEL ● ● ○

SIZE
8in (20cm) wide and 71in (180cm) long (including pom-poms)

YARN
Giant yarn from Lauren Aston Designs (100% merino wool), 5½yd (5m) to 3½oz (100g)
    7oz (200g) in Granite (A)
    14oz (400g) in Oyster (B)
Jumbo yarn from Lauren Aston Designs (100% merino wool), 11yd (10m) to 3½oz (100g)
    1¾oz (50g) in Bright Pink (C)

NEEDLES
Pair of US 70 (40mm) knitting needles

OTHER MATERIALS AND EQUIPMENT
Sewing needle and thread to match yarns A and B
2in (5cm) pom-pom maker
Sharp scissors
Strong thread to tie up the pom-poms

GAUGE (TENSION)
Approximately 1½ stitches and 2 rows to 4in (10cm) over st st.

ABBREVIATIONS
See page 92.

FOR THE SCARF
Cast on 3 sts in A.
Row 1: Knit.
Row 2: Purl.
Rows 3–10: Rep rows 1–2.
Change to B.
Rows 11–30: Rep rows 1–2.
Bind (cast) off.

TO MAKE UP
With your hands, weave in the loose ends and then stitch them neatly in place with the sewing needle and thread (see page 105).

Following the instructions that come with the pom-pom maker, make eight pom-poms in C, using strong thread to tie them around the middle. Sew four pom-poms across each end of the scarf, spacing them evenly.

Fun, fast, and with a pop of bright color, you can't go wrong with these chunky-knit—and super-snug—mittens. To go with these mitts you could make the Color-block Giant-knit Scarf (see page 10) in matching colors; they work brilliantly together.

Chunky-knit Pom-pom Mitts

SKILL LEVEL ● ● ○

SIZE
4¼in (11cm) wide (at widest part across flat hand) and 9½in (24cm) long

YARN
Super Chunky yarn from Lauren Aston Designs (100% merino wool), 71yd (65m) to 3½oz (100g)
   4½oz (130g) in Mid Grey (A)
Jumbo yarn from Lauren Aston Designs (100% merino wool), 11yd (10m) to 3½oz (100g)
   ¾oz (20g) in Bright Pink (B)

NEEDLES
Pair of US 15 (10mm) knitting needles
Large darning needle

OTHER MATERIALS AND EQUIPMENT
Stitch marker
Stitch holder
2¾in (7cm) pom-pom maker
Sharp scissors
Strong thread to tie up the pom-poms

GAUGE (TENSION)
Approximately 10 stitches and 19 rows to 4in (10cm) over garter st.

ABBREVIATIONS
See page 92.

FOR THE MITTS

BOTH MITTENS
Cast on 20 sts in A.
Rows 1–7: [K1, p1] to end of row.
Row 8: Inc, knit to end of row. (*21 sts*)
Rows 9–20: Knit.

LEFT-HAND MITTEN
Row 21: K8, inc, place stitch marker, inc, knit to end of row. (*23 sts*)

RIGHT-HAND MITTEN
Row 21: K11, inc, place stitch marker, inc, knit to end of row. (*23 sts*)

BOTH MITTENS
Rows 22: Knit.
Row 23: Knit and inc either side of the stitch marker. (*25 sts*)
Row 24: Knit.

LEFT-HAND MITTEN
Row 25: Knit to 3 sts before marker, place 7 sts on holder, pull yarn tight to draw rem sts up to sts knitted, knit to end of row. (*18 sts*)

RIGHT-HAND MITTEN
Row 25: Knit to 4 sts before marker, place 7 sts on holder, pull yarn tight to draw rem sts up to sts knitted, knit to end of row. (*18 sts*)

BOTH MITTENS
Rows 26–44: Knit.
Row 45: [K2tog] to end of row. (*9 sts*)
Cut the yarn and, starting at the other end, thread it through rem sts to create a circle of sts, then pull tight and sew in end (see page 105).

THUMB
Starting on a wrong side row.
Row 1: Using A, pick up and knit 1 st from side of holder, knit 7 sts from holder, pick up and knit 1 st from side of holder. (*9 sts*)
Rows 2–8: Knit.
Row 9: [K2tog] to last st, k1. (*5 sts*)
Cut the yarn and, starting at the other end, thread it through rem sts to create a circle of sts then pull tight to cinch together and sew in end (see page 105).

TO MAKE UP
Mattress stitch (see page 104) the thumb and side seams.
  Following the instructions that come with the pom-pom maker, make two pom-poms from B, using strong thread to tie them around the middle. Sew one to the back of each mitten, around the 10th row of garter stitch.

This sweet little headband makes a lovely gift, and it's wonderfully quick and easy to make. Whether it's used when applying make-up, warming your ears on a chilly day, or simply as a colorful accessory all day long, it's cozy and fun. Both the textured stitch pattern and the twist add lovely details to a really simple, classic design.

Twisted Headband

SKILL LEVEL ● ◉ ◉

SIZE
2¾in (7cm) wide and to fit head measuring 21–24in (53-63cm) in circumference

YARN
Super Chunky yarn from Lauren Aston Designs (100% merino wool), 71yd (65m) to 3½oz (100g)
   1oz (30g) in Light Grey
OR
   1oz (30g) in Heather

NEEDLES
Pair of US 13 (9mm) knitting needles
Large darning needle

GAUGE (TENSION)
Approximately 10 stitches and 14 rows to 4in (10cm) over pattern.

ABBREVIATIONS
See page 92.

NOTES
The best way to calculate the length of knitting is to measure your head (or the head of the person who will be wearing the band), and then deduct 1¼in (3cm) from that figure. If you can't measure the recipient's head, the average head circumference is around 21in (53cm), so your knitting would measure 20in (50cm).

FOR THE HEADBAND
Cast on 7 sts.
Row 1: [K1, p1] to last st, k1.
Row 1 sets seed (moss) stitch pattern and is repeated until work measures desired length (mine was 20in/50cm, which worked out to be 70 rows).
Bind (cast) off.

TO MAKE UP
Sew in loose ends (see page 105).
   Lay the piece flat, then lift one short end and flip it over so that the other side of the knitting is facing you. Keeping this twist in the knitting, flat stitch (see page 105) the short ends together as neatly as possible (they will be the back of the headband, sitting at the nape of the neck), and push the twist around to the front of the headband.

The beauty of this triangular-shaped wrap—both to look at and to knit—is in its simplicity. The bold shape is created quickly and easily using a simple technique that also creates the pattern of decorative holes along the sides. The tassel at the point and the braided ties are easy to make and help soften the overall look, making the wrap both cozy and stylish: a great accessory that's easy to wear.

Triangular Wrap

SKILL LEVEL ● ● ○

SIZE
Approximately 38in (97cm) wide (at widest point) and 20in (50cm) from top edge to point

YARN
Jumbo yarn from Lauren Aston Designs (100% merino wool), 11yd (10m) to 3½oz (100g)
  23oz (650g) in Mid Grey

NEEDLES
Pair of US 50 (25mm) knitting needles

GAUGE (TENSION)
Approximately 3 stitches and 5 rows to 4in (10cm) over garter st.

ABBREVIATIONS
See page 92.

FOR THE WRAP
Cast on 2 sts.
Row 1: K1, yo, k1.
Row 2: K1, yo, k2.
Row 3: K1, yo, knit to end.
Rows 4–25: Rep row 3.
Bind (cast) off, leaving a tail approx 1yd (1m) long.

TO MAKE UP
Trim loose end from cast on and fluff out the yarn to make a tassel.
  Cut a strand of yarn around 2yd (2m) long and thread it through the last bound (cast) off stitch so that you have three 1yd (1m) strands (including the tail from the bind/cast off). Braid the three strands and knot the end of the braid.
  Cut another 2yd (2m) strand of yarn and thread it through the corner opposite the first braid so you have two 1yd (1m) strands. Cut a final strand around 44in (120cm) and thread 8in (20cm) of it through the same place. Braid the three strands, incorporating the short end in with one of the longer strands.

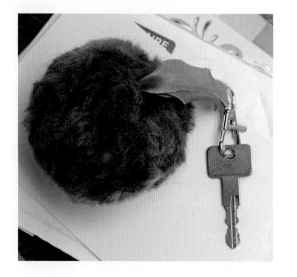

You'll never lose your keys again with these huge pom-pom keyrings! As with the pom-pom decorations (see pages 60 and 80), they're great for using up leftover yarn, and for creating a colorful and fun gift for yourself or someone else. The keyrings are quick, easy, and impactful, and a great project to make with children.

Pom-pom Keyrings

SKILL LEVEL ● ● ●

SIZE
Single pom-pom measures approx 3in (8cm) diameter and hangs about 5in (13cm) including the ribbon
Triple pom-pom measures approx 2¼in (6cm) diameter and hangs approx 9in (23cm) including the ribbon

YARN
Jumbo yarn from Lauren Aston Designs (100% merino wool), 11yd (10m) to 3½oz (100g)
   OR
Giant yarn from Lauren Aston Designs (100% merino wool), 5½yd (5m) to 3½oz (100g)
   ³⁄₈oz (10g) Teal for single pom-pom
   ¼oz (5g) each of Coral, Lilac, and Pewter Brown for triple pom-pom

OTHER MATERIALS AND EQUIPMENT
2¾in (7cm) pom-pom maker
2in (5cm) pom-pom maker
Sharp scissors
Strong thread to tie up the pom-poms
Ribbon (I used Habotai Silk Natural-Dyed Ribbon in Silver Mica, ⁵⁄₈in/1.6cm wide, by Lancaster and Cornish)
Keyring lobster clasp
Embroidery needle (for the triple pom-pom)

FOR THE SINGLE POM-POM KEYRING
Following the 2¾in (7cm) pom-pom maker instructions, wrap the yarn around one side of the maker and then the other, then cut the yarn down the middle of each wrap. Use the strong thread to tie the pom-pom very firmly and securely around the middle. Leave the ends of the thread long. Cut a piece of ribbon about 8in (20cm) long, thread it through the bottom loop of the lobster clasp and knot the ends together. Pass the long ends of the strong thread through the circle of ribbon and pull the knot in the ribbon as close to the center of the pom-pom as possible. Knot the thread tightly again to secure the ribbon. Open the pom-pom maker and trim the pom-pom to a neat(ish) round shape. It's quite tricky to trim the pom-poms very neatly, but personally I like them a little choppy to show the hand-made quality.

FOR THE TRIPLE POM-POM KEYRING
Following the 2in (5cm) pom-pom maker instructions, wrap the yarn around one side of the maker and then the other, then cut the yarn down the middle of each wrap. Use the strong thread to tie the pom-pom very firmly and securely around the middle. Open the pom-pom maker and trim the pom-pom to a neat(ish) round shape. It's quite tricky to trim the pom-poms very neatly, but personally I like them a little choppy to show the hand-made quality. Make the middle and bottom pom-poms in this way.

  For the top pom-pom, wrap and tie the yarn in the same way, but leave the ends of the thread long. Cut a piece of ribbon about 8in (20cm) long, thread it through the bottom loop of the lobster clasp and knot the ends together. Pass the long ends of the thread through the circle of ribbon and pull the knot in the ribbon as close to the center of the pom-pom as possible. Knot the thread tightly again to secure the ribbon, then open the pom-pom maker and trim the pom-pom.

Using an embroidery needle threaded with a long piece of strong thread, stitch through the center of all three pom-poms to join them together; go back and forth twice to ensure they're secure, then neatly knot the ends of the thread together and trim them.

Bramble stitch is such a lovely textured stitch, especially in a chunky yarn. It's also very repetitive and so easier to knit than it looks—perfect for knitting away while watching TV or having a chat. I particularly love using textured stitches in a dark-colored yarn because it means you need to look a little closer to see the detail, and then you really concentrate on it. And what better way to emphasize texture than to layer it up by wrapping the snood around more than once.

Bramble-stitch Snood

SKILL LEVEL ● ● ◌

SIZE
51in (130cm) long x 8¾in (22cm) wide (wraps around twice)

YARN
Super Chunky yarn from Lauren Aston Designs (100% merino wool), 71yd (65m) to 3½oz (100g)
  7oz (200g) in Damson

NEEDLES
Pair of US 17 (12mm) knitting needles
Large darning needle

GAUGE (TENSION)
Approximately 10 stitches and 13 rows to 4in (10cm) over pattern.

ABBREVIATIONS
See page 92.

FOR THE SNOOD
Cast on 22 sts.
Row 1: Purl.
Row 2: K1, *(k1, p1, k1 all into same st), p3tog; rep from * to last st, k1.
Row 3: Purl.
Row 4: K1, *p3tog, (k1, p1, k1 all into same st); rep from * to last st, k1.
Rows 5–100: Rep rows 1–4 (or cont in patt until knitting is desired length).
Bind (cast) off.

TO MAKE UP
Mattress stitch (see page 104) the cast-on and bound- (cast-) off ends together.

I love a clutch purse, and nothing makes me happier than a mixture of simple stitches and a pop of color. This little clutch combines simple techniques and stitches to create fun patterns and textures that work well together. I chose to line it with a contrasting fabric so that I can keep heavier items in it without it stretching out of shape, but you don't have to do that if you don't fancy it.

Chevron-edge Clutch Purse

SKILL LEVEL ● ● ○

SIZE
When closed the clutch measures approximately 9½in (24cm) wide and 7in (18cm) tall

YARN
Big Wool from Rowan (100% wool), 87yd (80m) to 3½oz (100g)
   1 ball in Concrete
1½yd (1.5m) of yarn in another color (I used Jumbo yarn from Lauren Aston Designs in Lilac)

NEEDLES
Pair of US 15 (10mm) knitting needles
Large darning needle
US P/16 (15mm) crochet hook (optional)

OTHER MATERIALS
Fat quarter of fabric for lining
Sewing needle and thread to match fabric

GAUGE (TENSION)
Approximately 9 stitches and 20 rows to 4in (10cm) over pattern.

ABBREVIATIONS
See page 92.

FOR THE PURSE

CHEVRON FRONT
Cast on 11 sts.
Row 1: Inc, knit to end of row. (*12 sts*)
Row 2: Knit.
Rows 3–8: Rep rows 1–2. (*15 sts*)
Row 9: K2tog, knit to end of row. (*14 sts*)
Row 10: Knit.
Rows 11–16: Rep rows 9–10. (*11 sts*)
Rows 17–48: Rep rows 1–16 twice more to make three points.
Bind (cast) off.

MAIN PURSE
Beg at back top edge, cast on 22 sts.
Rows 1–2: Knit.
Row 3: Purl.
Rows 4–10: Knit.
Row 11: Purl.
Rows 12–51: Rep rows 4–11.
Rows 52–55: Knit.
Bind (cast) off.

TO MAKE THE CHAIN
Split the contrast yarn lengthwise into two strands and discard one strand. Tie a slip knot at the end of the other strand, leaving a short tail. Create a chain either with your fingers or a US P/16 (15mm) crochet hook; pull the working yarn through the slip knot to make a loop, then pull the working yarn through that loop and repeat until the chain measures around 10in (25cm). Knot the end, leaving a short tail.

TO MAKE UP
If you're making a lining for your purse, fold the knitted main purse piece in half lengthwise and use that as a template to cut two pieces of fabric. Stitch the pieces of fabric right sides together along the sides and bottom seams, then turn under and sew a narrow hem around the top open edge to neaten it.
   Fold the knitted main purse in half lengthwise, wrong sides together. Place the chain across the front, about a third of the way down from the top. Keeping the chain in place, fold the purse right sides together and stitch the side seams closed, catching the ends of the chain tightly in place; you can then use the tails to knot it in place neatly on the inside.

Turn the purse the right way out with the chain on the front. If you're adding a lining, then place it inside the purse so that all the seams are hidden and the neat fabric edges are just below the top edge of the knitting, and hand stitch it in place.

Finally, mattress stitch (see page 104) the chevron front piece to the back edge of the purse opening. Tuck the chevron underneath the chain to close the purse.

This neutral bobble hat is both stylish and cozy—perfect for keeping you warm in winter—and the pewter brown complements so many other colors that the hat will go with almost everything. The simple repetitive pattern is easy to remember, making this a relatively easy and quick project to knit. You could add a hint of fun with a brightly colored pom-pom, or change the colors altogether if neutral isn't your style.

Bobble Hat

SKILL LEVEL ● ● ○

SIZE
Length (with brim cuff folded up and including pom-pom) 14¾in (37cm)
Circumference 18½in (47cm) stretching to 25½in (65cm)

YARN
Super Chunky yarn from Lauren Aston Designs (100% merino wool), 71yd (65m) to 3½oz (100g)
   2¾oz (80g) in Pewter Brown (A)
Jumbo yarn from Lauren Aston Designs (100% merino wool), 5½yd (5m) to 3½oz (100g)
   ⅜oz (10g) in Mink Blush (B)

NEEDLES
US 15 (10mm) circular knitting needle, 20in (50cm) long
Large darning needle

OTHER MATERIALS AND EQUIPMENT
Stitch marker
2¾in (7cm) pom-pom maker
Sharp scissors
Strong thread to tie up the pom-pom

GAUGE (TENSION)
Approximately 9 stitches and 30 rows to 4in (10cm) over pattern.

ABBREVIATIONS
See page 92.

FOR THE HAT
Cast on 32 sts in A.
Making sure the cast-on is not twisted, join it into a circle and place the stitch marker to mark the beginning of the round.
Rounds 1–6: [K2, p2] to end of round.
Round 7: Purl all stitches (this round will help encourage the brim of your hat to fold up on itself so you'll get a nice even cuff all round).
Rounds 8–35: [K2, p2] to end of round.
Round 36: [K2tog, p2] to end of round. *(24 sts)*
Round 37: [K1, p2tog] to end of round. *(16 sts)*
Cut yarn leaving a 6in (15cm) tail.
Thread tail through rem sts and pull tight, then secure.

TO MAKE UP
Stitch all loose ends into the inside of the hat (see page 105).
  Following the instructions that come with the pom-pom maker, make a pom-pom from B. Use the strong thread to tie up the pom-pom and to sew it to the top of the hat.

I'm a big fan of faux fur cuffs so I thought I'd make some in yarn, and I absolutely love them! I think they look wonderful with a good coat, they're perfect to wear for a day out, on the way to dinner, or at a winter wedding. So quick to make and such a small project, they're ideal for using up leftover wool you may have from other makes. I opted for a pewter brown pair as it goes with so many colors, but they'd also look amazing as a pop of coral or red.

Jumbo Cuffs

SKILL LEVEL ● ● ●

SIZE
4in (10cm) wide and to fit wrist measuring 5–8¾in (13–22cm) in circumference

YARN
Jumbo yarn from Lauren Aston Designs (100% merino wool), 11yd (10m) to 3½oz (100g)
  2oz (60g) in Pewter Brown (per cuff)

NEEDLES
Pair of US 50 (25mm) knitting needles

OTHER EQUIPMENT
Sewing needle and thread to match yarn

GAUGE (TENSION)
Approximately 3 stitches and 4 rows to 4in (10cm) over garter st.

ABBREVIATIONS
See page 92.

FOR EACH CUFF
Cast on 7 sts.
Rows 1–3: Knit.
Bind (cast) off.

TO MAKE UP
The bound- (cast-) off edge is on the inside of the cuff.
  Mattress stitch (see page 104) the short ends together: this can be a little fiddly as the yarn is so chunky, but do the best you can and sew the loose ends inside (see page 105) so they don't stick out when the cuffs are worn.

Is there anything nicer than snuggling up with a cup of tea and wearing your cozies? These socks were designed with that in mind; super-chunky and mega-cozy, they are perfect for lounging about and staying warm. Using a different technique to standard socks, the heel is inserted at the end, making them slightly easier to knit. The socks can easily be adjusted to fit different-sized feet—simply measure your foot and knit to that length, leaving 2in (5cm) for the toe.

Lounge-about Socks

SKILL LEVEL ● ● ●

SIZE
10½in (27cm) from cuff to heel and 8in (20cm) from heel to toe, but pattern can be adjusted to fit any length foot

YARN
Super Chunky yarn from Lauren Aston Designs (100% merino wool), 71yd (65m) to 3½oz (100g)
    1½oz (40g) in Mid Grey (A)
    3½oz (100g) in Natural White (B)
    Approximately 2yd (2m) of waste yarn (C)

NEEDLES
Set of 4 US 15 (10mm) double-pointed knitting needles
Large darning needle

OTHER EQUIPMENT
Stitch marker

GAUGE (TENSION)
Approximately 10 stitches and 14 rows to 4in (10cm) over st st.

ABBREVIATIONS
See page 92.

FOR EACH SOCK
Cast on 18 sts in A.
Divide the sts equally between 3 needles (6 sts on each needle) and making sure the cast-on is not twisted, join it into a circle and place the stitch marker to mark the beginning of the round.
Rounds 1–6: Knit.
Join in B.
Rounds 7–32: Knit.
Round 33: Using just the 3 working needles, knit 5 stitches from N1 onto N3 (there should be 1 stitch left on N1), transfer 2 stitches from N3 onto N2 (current setup 1, 8, 9), then move 3 stitches from N2 onto N1. *(4, 5, 9 sts)*
Round 34: Using 4 needles again, N1 inc in first st then knit to end; N2 knit to last st, inc; N3 inc in first and last sts. *(5, 6, 11 sts)*

PREPARE HEEL
The 11 sts on N3 will be the heel and this will be completed later when the waste yarn is removed; for now, with RS facing, join in C and with the free needle knit all sts on N3, turn, purl all sts. This completes the preparation for the heel. Cont in B, knitting across all needles in rounds as before.
Round 35: N1 k2tog, then knit to end; N2 knit to last 2 sts, k2tog; N3 k2tog first 2 sts and last 2 sts. *(4, 5, 9 sts)*
Rounds 36–52: Knit. (This is where to adjust if you're making for a smaller or larger foot by knitting fewer or more rows. Allow 1½in/4cm for toe and 1¼in/3cm for heel, both yet to be worked.)
Change to A.
Round 53: Knit.

Arrange sts so that the N1 and N2 sts are on one needle and the rem 9 sts are on another needle.

Round 54: K2tog first 2 sts and last 2 sts on both needles, knitting all other sts.

Round 55: Knit.

Rounds 56–57: Rep rounds 54–55. (*10 sts*)

Cut yarn, thread through rem sts, and pull up and secure tightly to close hole.

KNITTING THE HEEL

Carefully cut between the 2 rows of C (waste yarn) and unravel, place original sts in B on a separate needle for each edge of the heel. Using A with RS facing, [pick up 1 st from corner of heel, 11 sts across sts on needle] twice. There will be 12 sts on each needle. (*24 sts in total*)

Spread the stitches over 3 needles 12, 6, 6, with the 12 stitches being the "underneath" of the sock (the sole of the foot).

Rounds 1–4: N1 k2tog, then knit to last 2 sts, k2tog; N2 k2tog then knit to end; N3 knit to last 2 sts, k2tog. (*8 sts*)

Cut yarn, thread through rem sts, and pull up and secure tightly to close hole.

TO MAKE UP

Sew in loose ends (see page 105).

Another quick knit with endless color options, this hat is a brilliant starter project to practice working on circular needles. There's no shaping involved, just rib and stockinette (stocking) stitch with some color changes. The hat uses three colors to knit with and a fourth for the pom-poms, so you could go as bright and bold as you fancy, or tone it down with multiple shades of one color.

Striped Square Hat

SKILL LEVEL ● ● ○

SIZE
8¾in (22cm) wide x 8¾in (22cm) tall, with brim folded up

YARN
Big Wool from Rowan (100% wool), 87yd (80m) to 3½oz (100g)
  2oz (60g) in Smokey (A)
Spuntaneous from Cascade Yarns (100% fine merino wool), 109yd (100m) 7oz (200g)
  1¼oz (35g) in Silver (B)
  1oz (30g) in Blue Coral (C)
Jumbo yarn from Lauren Aston Designs (100% merino wool), 11yd (10m) to 3½oz (100g)
  ¾oz (20g) in Mid Grey (D)

NEEDLES
US 15 (10mm) and US 17 (12mm) circular knitting needles, both 20in (50cm) long
Large darning needle

OTHER MATERIALS AND EQUIPMENT
2¾in (7cm) pom-pom maker
Sharp scissors
Strong thread to tie up the pom-poms

GAUGE (TENSION)
Approximately 8 stitches and 12 rows to 4in (10cm) over st st.

ABBREVIATIONS
See page 92.

FOR THE HAT
Using US 15 (10mm) circular knitting needle and A, cast on 36 sts.
Making sure the cast-on is not twisted, join it into a circle and place the stitch marker to mark the beginning of the round.
Rounds 1–7: [K2, p2] to end of row.
Round 8: Purl all stitches (this round will help encourage the brim of your hat to fold up on itself so you'll get a nice even cuff all round).
Change to US 17 (12mm) circular knitting needle.
Rounds 9–16: Knit.
Change to B.
Rounds 17–18: Knit.
Change to C.
Rounds 19–20: Knit.
Rounds 21–34: Rep rounds 17–20, keeping color changes as set.
Bind (cast) off evenly.

TO MAKE UP
Sew in loose ends (see page 105).
  Mattress stitch (see page 104) the bound- (cast-) off round together in a straight line to close the top of the hat. Fold up the rib at the purled round (round 8).
  Following the instructions that come with the pom-pom maker, make two pom-poms in D using strong thread to tie them around the middle. Sew one pom-pom to each of the corners at the top of the hat.

VARIATION

Pink and blue hat measures 8¾in (22cm) tall x 8in (20cm) wide

YARN

Big Wool from Rowan (100% wool), 87yd (80m) to 3½oz (100g)
  1¾oz (50g) in Ice Blue (A)
  1oz (30g) in Smoky (B)
  ¾oz (25g) in Prize (C)
Jumbo yarn from Lauren Aston Designs (100% merino wool), 11yd (10m) to 3½oz (100g)
  ¾oz (20g) in Coral (D)

GAUGE (TENSION)

Approximately 9 stitches and 12 rows to 4in (10cm) over st st.

Make up hat following main pattern.

I love a cozy snood that wraps around multiple times. You can wrap or unwrap layers depending on the temperature, and it looks so snug in winter. As ever, I've opted for two neutrals and a flash of color so that the snood will go with lots of outfits, and still have a little something different to add interest.

Color-block Snood

SKILL LEVEL ● ● ●

SIZE
Approximately 4¾in (12.5cm) wide x 74¾in (190cm) circumference

YARN
Magnum from Cascade Yarns (100% Peruvian Highland wool), 123yd (112m) to 8¾oz (250g)
4½oz (125g) in Ecru (A)
1oz (30g) in Poinsettia (B)
4½oz (125g) in Doeskin Heather (C)

NEEDLES
Pair of US 17 (12mm) knitting needles
Large darning needle

GAUGE (TENSION)
Approximately 8 stitches and 10 rows to 4in (10cm) over pattern.

ABBREVIATIONS
See page 92.

FOR THE SNOOD
Cast on 10 sts in A.
Rows 1–2: [K1, p1] to end of row.
Rows 3–4: [P1, k1] to end of row.
Rows 5–96: Rep rows 1–4.
Then rep rows 1–3 once.
Change to B.
Rows 100–119: Starting with a row 4, cont in patt as set, ending with a row 3.
Change to C.
Rows 120–190: Starting with a row 4, cont in patt as set, ending with a row 2.
Bind (cast) off evenly.

TO MAKE UP
Sew in loose ends (see page 105).
   Lay the knitting flat, fold it in half lengthwise and flip the top layer over so that there's a twist in the strip. Mattress stitch (see page 104) the cast-on and bound- (cast-) off ends together.

No more frozen fingers with this easy-to-wear cable-knit hand muff. Hand muffs are practical, cozy, and stylish (with the right pattern!); I love them for a winter wedding or a country walk instead of gloves. This simple repetitive pattern is a great introduction to cable knits, as it only uses the basics and the huge stitches make it easier than ever to see what you're doing.

Cable-knit Hand Muff

SKILL LEVEL ● ● ◌

SIZE
Approximately 14 x 10in (35 x 25cm) laid flat

YARN
Jumbo yarn from Lauren Aston Designs (100% merino wool), 11yd (10m) to 3½oz (100g)
   17½oz (500g) in Lilac

NEEDLES
Pair of US 50 (25mm) knitting needles
US 50 (25mm) cable needle

OTHER MATERIALS AND EQUIPMENT
Sewing needle and thread to match yarn
Approximately 1½yd (1.5m) of ribbon of your choice for strap

GAUGE (TENSION)
Approximately 3½ stitches and 3 rows to 4in (10cm) over pattern.

ABBREVIATIONS
See page 92.

FOR THE MUFF
Cast on 12 sts.
Row 1 (RS): P2, k8, p2.
Row 2 and every other WS row: Knit all knit stitches and purl all purl stitches.
Row 3: As row 1.
Row 5: P2, C4B, C4F, p2.
Rows 7–24: Rep rows 1–6.
Bind (cast) off.

TO MAKE UP
Sew in loose ends (see page 105).
   Mattress stitch (see page 104) the cast-on and bound- (cast-) off ends together.
   Thread the ribbon right through the muff and tie the ends together so that the muff sits at the height you would like.

I'm a firm believer in the benefits of a headband on a bad hair day, and this super-chunky turban-style version is very forgiving. Knit in simple stockinette (stocking) stitch, the edges begin to roll around on themselves, which works to create a really full effect. The way the band twists around itself like a pretzel is the key to how it looks, and also means it's lovely and toasty warm, so it's also great for keeping your ears snug on a dog walk.

Turban-style Headband

SKILL LEVEL ● ● ●

SIZE
3¼in (8.5cm) wide and to fit head measuring 21–24in (53–63cm) in circumference

YARN
Super Chunky yarn from Lauren Aston Designs (100% merino wool), 71yd (65m) to 3½oz (100g)
  2¾oz (80g) in Damson

NEEDLES
Pair of US 19 (15mm) knitting needles
Large darning needle

GAUGE (TENSION)
Approximately 7 stitches and 8 rows to 4in (10cm) over st st using yarn doubled.

ABBREVIATIONS
See page 92.

NOTES
The best way to calculate the length of knitting is to measure your head (or the head of the person who will be wearing the band) and then multiply that number by two and add 4in (10cm) for seams and overlap. If you can't measure the recipient's head, the average head circumference is around 21in (53cm), so your knitting would measure 21 (53) x 2 = 42 (106) + 4 (10) = 46 (116).

FOR THE HEADBAND
Using both ends of yarn held together as one strand throughout, cast on 6 sts.
Row 1: Knit.
Row 2: Purl.
Rep rows 1–2 until work measures desired length (mine was 45¼in/115cm, which worked out to be 92 rows).
Bind (cast) off.

TO MAKE UP
Sew in loose ends (see page 105) and steam the knitting as flat as possible.
  Flat stitch (see page 105) the short ends together so that the knitting is a large circle and lay it on a flat surface.
  Pick up the seam and twist the circle in the middle to create a figure-eight. Fold the figure-eight in half at the twist so that you have two circles, one on top of the other. The seam will be on the upper circle.
  Spin the piece around so that the seam is closest to you. With your right hand, pick up the top piece on the right of the circle and fold it in half over to the left, so you have three pieces on the left-hand side and one piece on the right-hand side. With your left hand, pinch together the top and bottom pieces on the inside of the circle, and with your right hand pull the middle piece to the outside of the circle and then over to the right. The two circles should now be linked together on one side of the circle, with the seam on the other side. You may want to stitch the two pieces together close to the seam to keep them in place so the headband is quick and easy to put on in future.

These slipper socks are knit with a heel, making them a mix of both mega-cozy socks and little boot-style slippers. They have the best elements of both, with the flexibility of a sock and the warmth and style of a slipper. Because both the yarn and needles are so big, the slipper socks are ideally worn with ordinary socks to work as a lining and keep you super-cozy. Perfect for lazy winter days lounging around the house. The needles can be a little hard to hold to begin with, but since the socks are fast to knit, it's not difficult for long.

Super-snug Slipper Socks

SKILL LEVEL ● ● ●

SIZE
10¼in (26cm) along the sole and 16in (40cm) from heel to cuff

YARN
Collection Wool Yarn from Lion Brand (100% wool), 22yd (20m) to 7oz (200g)
   21oz (600g) in Cream

NEEDLES
Set of 4 US 50 (25mm) double-pointed knitting needles
Large darning needle

OTHER MATERIALS AND EQUIPMENT
Stitch marker
2 pieces of felt in the color of your choice, each measuring approx 8 x 4in (20 x 10cm)
Non-slip glue or pads
Sewing needle and threads to match yarn, and to match (or contrast with) the felt color

GAUGE (TENSION)
Approximately 3½ stitches and 5 rows to 4in (10cm) over pattern.

ABBREVIATIONS
See page 92.

NOTES
The pattern is written to fit US size 6½–8½ (UK4–6) feet. If you need to make them smaller or larger, you can add or decrease rounds between rounds 26–31 in the pattern, bearing in mind that 1 row will alter length by around ¾in (2cm).

FOR EACH SOCK

Cast on 8 sts.

Divide the sts between 3 needles (2, 4, 2) and making sure the cast-on is not twisted, join it into a circle and place the stitch marker to mark the beginning of the round.

Rounds 1–15: Knit.

SHAPE HEEL

Working back and forth in rows on 2 needles, cont as folls:

Row 16: K6, turn.

Row 17: P4, turn.

Row 18: K4, turn.

Row 19: P4, turn.

Row 20: K1, k2tog, k1, turn.

Row 21: P1, p2tog, turn. *(6 sts in total)*

Row 22: Knit across rem 2 sts on needle, pick up and knit 3 sts along side of heel, k2 on next needle.

Cont in rounds.

Round 23: K2, pick up and knit 3 sts along side of heel (opposite side of the heel to where the sts were picked up on row 22). *(12 sts)*

Stitches on needles should now be 5, 2, 5, spread stitches evenly by slipping 1 stitch from the first and third needle (each with 5 stitches) onto either end of the second needle so there are 4 sts on each needle.

Round 24: [K1, k2tog, k1] to end of round. *(9 sts)*

Round 25: K1, k2tog, k4, k2tog. *(7 sts)*

Rounds 26–31: Knit (this is where you can alter the number of rows to change the size of the socks).

Round 32: K2tog, k3, k2tog. *(5 sts)*

Cut yarn, thread through rem sts, and pull up and secure tightly to close hole.

TO MAKE UP

Sew in loose ends (see page 105).

Cut the felt pieces into ovals approximately 8in (20cm) long by 3¾in (9.5cm) wide (or the size needed to fit the sole of the socks).

Place one felt piece over the sole of each slipper and hand stitch them in position. I used two strands of thread and a criss-cross stitch to make the sewing a little stronger and also decorative, but you can use any stitch you like as long as it's secure.

Once both slippers have had the soles stitched onto them, apply the non-slip glue to the felt. I put mine on in dots all over the soles, but you can draw anything you fancy so why not get creative? Let the glue dry.

You can fold the cuffs over to make little booties or leave them long if you prefer.

This huge scarf will keep you cozy in winter and can be made in any mixture of colors to be as vibrant or neutral as you like, depending on your personal style. It's a real statement that's brilliant fun with heaps of texture.

Giant Pom-pom Scarf

SKILL LEVEL ● ● ●

SIZE
67 x 6¼in (170 x 16cm)

YARN
Jumbo yarn from Lauren Aston Designs (100% merino wool), 11yd (10m) to 3½oz (100g)
  4yd (4m) in Mid Grey (A)
Jumbo yarn from Lauren Aston Designs (100% merino wool), 11yd (10m) to 3½oz (100g)
OR
Giant yarn from Lauren Aston Designs (100% merino wool), 5½yd (5m) to 3½oz (100g)
  5¼oz (150g) each of Oyster, Light Grey, Mid Grey, Granite, Baby Blue, and Midnight

OTHER MATERIALS AND EQUIPMENT
2¾in (7cm) pom-pom maker
3½in (9cm) pom-pom maker
Sharp scissors
Strong thread to tie up the pom-poms, ideally to match yarn A

FOR THE SCARF
You need to make around 50 pom-poms in a variety of colors and sizes: I used 6 colors of yarn and 2 sizes of pom-pom maker.

Following the pom-pom maker instructions, wrap the yarn around one side of the maker and then the other, then cut the yarn down the middle of each wrap. Use the strong thread to tie the pom-pom very firmly and securely around the middle. Leave the ends of the thread long. Open the pom-pom maker and trim the pom-pom to a neat(ish) round shape. It's quite tricky to trim the pom-poms very neatly, but personally I like them a little choppy to show the hand-made quality.

TO MAKE UP
Using Jumbo yarn in A (or the color you think will work best as a base if you are using different colors), create a slip knot close to one end. Pull the working yarn through the slip knot to make a loop, then pull the working yarn through that loop and repeat until the chain measures 63in (160cm): this is the skeleton for the scarf.

Lay the skeleton chain out flat on a desk or floor and begin to tie the pom-poms to it, using the long ends you left when making the pom-poms. Alternatively, you can easily sew the pom-poms to the scarf, it just takes a little longer. I started with one color of pom-poms and tied them on at random intervals along the chain, and then moved to the next color, repeating this and gradually filling in the gaps. You may want to make more pom-poms and fill out the chain even more depending on how it looks as you are tying them on.

These fingerless gloves are ideal for spring and fall. They're fast to make and include a quirky little sewn stitch in a contrasing color, which is for both style and practicality—so you can fix the opening to suit your hands. As always, you could make them in the colors of your choice: I love a warm purple, and when it comes to purple, you can never go wrong with a splash or stripe of mustard yellow.

Striped Fingerless Gloves

SKILL LEVEL ● ● ○

SIZE
3in (8cm) wide across flat hand x 7in (18cm) long

YARN
Super Chunky yarn from Lauren Aston Designs (100% merino wool), 71yd (65m) to 3½oz (100g)
   1½oz (40g) in Heather (A)
   ⅜oz (10g) in Mustard (B)
   Small amount of Light Grey for decorative stitching

NEEDLES
Set of 4 US 15 (10mm) double-pointed knitting needles
Large darning needle

OTHER EQUIPMENT
Stitch marker

GAUGE (TENSION)
Approximately 10 stitches and 13 rows to 4in (10cm) over pattern.

ABBREVIATIONS
See page 92.

FOR EACH GLOVE
Cast on 12 sts in A.
Divide the sts equally between 3 needles and making sure the cast-on is not twisted, join it into a circle and place the stitch marker to mark the beginning of the round.
Rounds 1–6: Knit.
Round 7: Inc in first st on every needle. (*15 sts*)
Change to B.
Round 8: Knit.
Change to A.
Rounds 9–10: Knit.
Change to B.
Rep rounds 8–10 once more.
DIVIDE FOR THUMB
Change to B.
Round 14: Turn the work and purl all sts.
Change to A.
Round 15: Turn the work and knit all sts.
Round 16: Turn the work and purl all sts.
Change to B.
Round 17: Turn the work and knit all sts.
Change to A.
Round 18: Turn the work and purl all sts.
Round 19: Turn the work and knit all sts.

Change to B.
Round 20: Join the gap by returning to working in the round, and knit all sts.
Change to A.
Rounds 21–22: Knit.
Round 23: K2tog first 2 sts on every needle. (*12 sts*)
Round 24: Knit.
Bind (cast) off.

TO MAKE UP
Sew in loose ends (see page 105). Using Light Grey yarn, make a couple of straight stitches across the bottom of the opening (near to round 15 or 16, depending on how open/closed you want the thumb gap to be).

CHAPTER TWO

For the Home

All of these homeware projects were designed with cozy nesting in mind. The giant stitches add amazing texture and comfort, making a real statement. There's an underlying Scandinavian feel to many of the knits, emphasized by the subtle colors, which are then brought out of their shell with pops of brighter shades. These accents are perfect for mixing and matching to the colors of your home. The patterns vary in difficulty, but the great thing is that some of the easiest makes have the most impact.

For beginners, why not start with the Blanket-stitched Pillow (see page 52), or the Pom-pom Trim Blanket (see page 68) for quick-and-easy statement pieces. Seasoned knitters should also enjoy the challenge of giant knitting—the Giant Cable Blanket (see page 86) is perfect for WOW factor, and the Hanging Plant Pot Holder (see page 74) makes a beautiful gift.

I don't do a lot of arm knitting, but it is fun to dabble every now and again. It's really easy to create a simple arm-knitted blanket in classic stockinette (stocking) stitch, so I wanted to mix it up a little by adding a twist to the stitches to create a more interesting finish.

The thing to remember about arm knitting is that while you are doing it you can't really do anything else. For this reason I like to begin and end an arm knitting project within an hour, which is very doable for a blanket this size. My top tip is to keep a broomstick nearby to transfer your stitches onto in case the doorbell rings!

Twisted Stitch Arm-knit Blanket

SKILL LEVEL ● ● ◉

SIZE
31½ x 36½in (80 x 93cm)

YARN
Giant yarn from Lauren Aston Designs (100% merino wool), 5½yd (5m) to 3½oz (100g)
53oz (1.5kg) in Buttermilk

NEEDLES
This project is arm-knitted

OTHER EQUIPMENT
Sewing needle and thread to match yarn

GAUGE (TENSION)
Approximately 1½ stitches and 1½ rows to 4in (10cm) over st st.

ABBREVIATIONS
See page 92.

NOTES
See page 106 for instructions for arm knitting.

FOR THE BLANKET
Cast on 12 sts.

Arm knit 14 rows, twisting every stitch by pulling the yarn through the stitch on your working arm to create the new stitch, then inserting your second hand through the back of the new stitch so that your knuckles meet and placing the stitch onto your other arm.

To bind (cast) off, make sure you have enough yarn left: you need around 5 times the length of your knitting so, as this blanket is 31½in (80cm) wide, you'll need around 4½yd (4m) of working yarn. Be sure to bind (cast) off very loosely.

TO MAKE UP
Sew in loose ends (see page 105).

This fun double-sided pillow uses a mixture of simple stitches to great effect. It is also a nice introduction to blanket stitch, which is easy to work neatly between the knitted stitches. To keep the pillow from being over-the-top I used two different shades of gray for the main panels and a pop of coral for the blanket-stitched edge.

Blanket-stitched Pillow

SKILL LEVEL ● ● ●

SIZE
17½ x 17½in (44 x 44cm)

YARN
Jumbo yarn from Lauren Aston Designs (100% merino wool), 11yd (10m) to 3½oz (100g)
   14oz (400g) in Light Grey (A)
   14oz (400g) in Mid Grey (B)
   3½oz (100g) in Coral (C)

NEEDLES
Pair of US 50 (25mm) knitting needles

OTHER MATERIALS
15 x 15in (40 x 40cm) pillow pad

GAUGE (TENSION)
Approximately 2½ stitches and 4 rows to 4in (10cm) over both patterns.

ABBREVIATIONS
See page 92.

FOR THE PILLOW
SIDE 1
Cast on 11 sts in A.
Row 1: Knit.
Row 2: Purl.
Rows 3–16: Rep rows 1–2.
Bind (cast) off.
SIDE 2
Cast on 11 sts in B.
Row 1: [K1, p1] to end of row.
Rows 2–16: Rep row 1.
Bind (cast) off.

TO MAKE UP
Tuck in loose ends.
  Lay both pieces flat one on top of each other with wrong sides together. Work blanket stitch (see page 105) around three sides, using your fingers rather than a needle because the yarn is so thick.
  Place the pillow pad inside and blanket stitch the last side of the knitting closed.

These sweet little Christmas trees look great on the mantle, coffee table, or even as a centerpiece (especially mixed with some pine cones). Each of the patterns can be scaled up or down simply by altering the amount of stitches you cast on with, so you can create your own forest of Christmas trees in no time!

Knitted Christmas Trees

SKILL LEVEL ● ● ◌

SIZE
Tree 1: 9in (23cm) tall x 4in (10cm) diameter at base, weighs 1¾oz (50g)
Tree 2: 6¼in (16cm) tall x 2½in (6cm) diameter at base, weighs ¾oz (25g)
Tree 3: 8¾in (22cm) tall x 2in (5cm) diameter at base, weighs ¾oz (25g)
Tree 4: 7¼in (18cm) tall x 3½in (9cm) diameter at base, weighs 1oz (30g)
Tree 5: 4¾in (12cm) tall x 2in (5cm) diameter at base, weighs ³⁄₈oz (15g)

YARN
Magnum from Cascade Yarns (100% Peruvian highland wool), 123yd (112m) to 8¾oz (250g)
 5oz (140g) in Shire

NEEDLES
Set of 4 US 17 (12mm) double-pointed knitting needles
Large darning needle

OTHER EQUIPMENT
Stitch marker

GAUGE (TENSION)
Approximately 7 stitches and 10 rows to 4in (10cm) over st st.

ABBREVIATIONS
See page 92.

Opposite, left to right: Tree 2, tree 4, tree 3, tree 1, and tree 5.

FOR TREE 1
Cast on 22 sts.
Divide the sts between 3 needles and making sure the cast-on is not twisted, join it into a circle and place the stitch marker to mark the beginning of the round.
Round 1: Purl.
Rounds 2–3: Knit.
Round 4: P2tog, p12, p2tog, p6. *(20 sts)*
Rounds 5–6: Knit.
Round 7: P2tog, p11, p2tog, p5. *(18 sts)*
Rounds 8–9: Knit.
Round 10: P2tog, p10, p2tog, p4. *(16 sts)*
Rounds 11–12: Knit.
Round 13: P2tog, p9, p2tog, p3. *(14 sts)*
Rounds 14–15: Knit.
Round 16: P2tog, p7, p2tog, p3. *(12 sts)*
Rounds 17–18: Knit.
Round 19: P2tog, p6, p2tog, p2. *(10 sts)*
Rounds 20–21: Knit.
Round 22: P2tog, p5, p2tog, p1. *(8 sts)*
Rounds 23–24: Knit.
Round 25: P2tog, p3, p2tog, p1. *(6 sts)*
Rounds 26–27: Knit.
Round 28: P2tog, p2, p2tog. *(4 sts)*
Cut yarn, thread through rem sts, and pull up and secure tightly to close hole.

TO MAKE UP
For all trees, sew in loose ends (see page 105).

Rounds 12–13: Knit.
Round 14: K1, k2tog, k4. *(6 sts)*
Rounds 15–17: Knit.
Round 18: K2, k2tog, k2. *(5 sts)*
Round 19: Knit.
Round 20: K2tog, k3. *(4 sts)*
Round 21: Knit.
Round 22: K2, k2tog. *(3 sts)*
Round 23: Knit.
Cut yarn, thread through rem sts, and pull up and secure tightly to close hole.

FOR TREE 4

Cast on 18 sts.
Divide the sts between 3 needles and making sure the cast-on is not twisted, join it into a circle and place the stitch marker to mark the beginning of the round.
Round 1: Knit.
Round 2: Purl.
Rounds 3–4: Knit.
Round 5: [K2tog, k4] 3 times. *(15 sts)*
Rounds 6–7: Knit.
Round 8: [K2tog, k3] 3 times. *(12 sts)*
Rounds 9–10: Knit.
Round 11: [K2tog, k2] 3 times. *(9 sts)*
Rounds 12–13: Knit.
Round 14: [K2tog, k1] 3 times. *(6 sts)*
Rounds 15–16: Knit.
Round 17: [K2tog] 3 times. *(3 sts)*
Cut yarn, thread through rem sts, and pull up and secure tightly to close hole.

FOR TREE 2

Cast on 14 sts.
Divide the sts between 3 needles and making sure the cast-on is not twisted, join it into a circle and place the stitch marker to mark the beginning of the round.
Round 1: Purl.
Rounds 2–3: Knit.
Round 4: P2tog, p7, p2tog, p3. *(12 sts)*
Rounds 5–6: Knit.
Round 7: P2tog, p6, p2tog, p2. *(10 sts)*
Rounds 8–9: Knit.
Round 10: P2tog, p5, p2tog, p1. *(8 sts)*
Rounds 11–12: Knit.
Round 13: P2tog, p3, p2tog, p1. *(6 sts)*
Rounds 14–15: Knit.
Round 16: P2tog, p2, p2tog. *(4 sts)*
Cut yarn, thread through rem sts, and pull up and secure tightly to close hole.

FOR TREE 3

Cast on 10 sts.
Divide the sts between 3 needles and making sure the cast-on is not twisted, join it into a circle and place the stitch marker to mark the beginning of the round.
Round 1: Knit.
Round 2: Purl.
Round 3: Knit.
Round 4: K4, k2tog, k4. *(9 sts)*
Rounds 5–6: Knit.
Round 7: K3, k2tog, k4. *(8 sts)*
Rounds 8–10: Knit.
Round 11: K1, k2tog, k5. *(7 sts)*

FOR TREE 5

Cast on 11 sts.
Divide the sts between 3 needles and making sure the cast-on is not twisted, join it into a circle and place the stitch marker to mark the beginning of the round.
Rounds 1–2: [K1, p1] to last st, k1.
Round 3: K2tog, k5, k2tog, k2. *(9 sts)*
Round 4 and foll alt rounds: As round 2.
Round 5: K2tog, k4, k2tog, k1. *(7 sts)*
Round 7: K2tog, k3, k2tog. *(5 sts)*
Round 9: K2tog, k1, k2tog. *(3 sts)*
Cut yarn, thread through rem sts, and pull up and secure tightly to close hole.

For me, nothing says Christmas like a stocking. The decorations just aren't complete until the stockings are hanging from the mantel or banister. I also love the Scandinavian-inspired Christmas decorations that have become popular, so I wanted to blend the themes of traditional and Scandi Christmas and create a lovely striped stocking. My favorite part about this stocking is that you can make it as many times as you like, changing the stripes each time to create a collection of stockings that work together, yet each one is slightly different.

Scandi Christmas Stocking

SKILL LEVEL ● ● ●

SIZE
17¾in (45cm) from cuff to heel and 8in (20cm) from heel to toe

YARN
Super Chunky yarn from Lauren Aston Designs (100% merino wool), 71yd (65m) to 3½oz (100g)
  3¼oz (90g) in Natural White (A)
  2¼oz (65g) in Mid Grey (B)

NEEDLES
US 15 (10mm) circular knitting needle, 20in (50cm) long
Large darning needle

OTHER EQUIPMENT
3 stitch markers (preferably all different so you can easily tell which is 1, 2, and 3)

GAUGE (TENSION)
Approximately 10 stitches and 13 rows to 4in (10cm) over st st.

ABBREVIATIONS
See page 92.

FOR THE STOCKING
Cast on 28 sts in A.
Making sure the cast-on is not twisted, join it into a circle and place a stitch marker to mark the beginning of the round.
Rounds 1–8: [K1, p1] to end of round.
Rounds 9–12: Knit in A.
Rounds 13–16: Knit in B.
Rounds 17–24: Knit in A.
Round 25: Knit in B.
Round 26: Knit in A.
Rounds 27–28: Knit in B.
Rounds 29–30: Knit in A.
Rounds 31–34: Knit in B.
Rounds 35–38: Knit in A.
Rounds 39–40: Knit in B.
Rounds 41–42: Knit in A.
Round 43: Knit in B.
Round 44: Knit in A.

SHAPE THE HEEL
Round 45: In A knit to last 7 sts, change to B, k7.
Cont in B for rest of heel.
Next row: K7, (so now 14 sts in B) turn, sl1 purlwise, p13; work on these 14 stitches only for the next 16 rows by turning the work at the end of each row as folls:
Next row: Sl1, k13, turn.
Next row: Sl1 purlwise, p13, turn.
Rep last 2 rows 3 times more.
Next row: Sl1, k13, turn.
Next row: Sl1 purlwise, p to last 3 sts, p2tog, p1, turn. *(13 sts)*
Next row: Sl1, k to last 3 sts, ssk, k1, turn. *(12 sts)*
Rep last 2 rows once more.
For the next three rows you'll be leaving 1 st unworked at the end of each row; include it in the stitch count but don't work it.

Next row: Sl1 purlwise, p to last 4 sts, p2tog, p1, turn leaving 1 st unworked. *(9 sts)*
Next row: Sl1, k to last 4 sts, ssk, k1, turn leaving 1 st unworked. *(8 sts)*
Next row: Sl1 purlwise, p to last 4 sts, p2tog, p1, turn leaving 1 st unworked. *(7 sts)*

HEEL GUSSET
Change to A.
Next round: Ignoring the unworked st, knit across 6 heel sts, then pick up and knit 8 sts from side of heel, k14 sts, pick up and knit another 8 sts from side of heel, k the unworked st and another 3 sts to center of heel. *(37 sts)*
Next round: Place stitch marker 1 (SM1), k11, place stitch marker 2 (SM2), k14, place stitch marker 3 (SM3), k12. (SM2 and SM3 mark gusset decrease points and SM1 is beg of round.)
Next round: Slip marker, knit to 3 sts before SM2, k2tog, k1, slip marker, knit to SM3, slip marker, k1, ssk, knit to SM1.
Rep this round twice more.
Change to B.
Next round: Knit to SM1, slip marker, knit to 3 sts before SM2, k2tog, k1, slip marker, knit to SM3, slip marker, k1, ssk, knit to SM1.
Next round: Knit in B (keeping stitch markers in place on this and foll rows).
Next 5 rounds: Knit in A.
Next round: Knit in B.
Next 2 rounds: Knit in A.
Next 2 rounds: Knit in B.
Next 2 rounds: Knit in A.
Change to B.

SHAPE TOE
Next round: Slip marker, knit to 3 sts before SM2, ssk, k1, slip marker, k1, k2tog, knit to 3 sts before SM3, ssk, k1, slip marker, k1, k2tog, knit to SM1.
Rep last round 3 times more.
Next round: Knit, removing markers as you go.
Cut yarn, thread through rem sts, and pull up and secure tightly to close hole.

TO MAKE UP
Sew in loose ends (see page 105).
  To make hanging loop, cut 3 strands of B each approximately 16in (40cm). Knot the strands loosely together at one end then braid them and knot the other end loosely. Thread the braid through the top of the stocking, undo the knots and tie both ends together to make a loop the desired length. Trim ends and pull the knot to inside the stocking, or to the top of the loop if you want it to show.

I absolutely love a pom-pom, and they are the perfect way to use up leftover yarn. These hanging decorations add texture and tactile aesthetic in any color you fancy. Red, white, and green on the Christmas tree, pops of color for a party, or simply colors to suit your décor for everyday enjoyment. All yarns produce a different finish, my favorite being these super-fluffy ones, but why not try mixing it up with other yarns for a range of textures and finishes?

Hanging Pom-pom Decorations

SKILL LEVEL ● ● ●

SIZE
Pom-pom measures around 3in (8cm) diameter and hangs about 5in (13cm) including ribbon

YARN
Jumbo yarn from Lauren Aston Designs (100% merino wool), 11yd (10m) to 3½oz (100g)
OR
Giant yarn from Lauren Aston Designs (100% merino wool), 5½yd (5m) to 3½oz (100g)
 ³⁄₈oz (10g) in each of Teal, Midnight, Mid Grey, Shadow, Pewter, and Mink

OTHER MATERIALS AND EQUIPMENT
2¾in (7cm) pom-pom maker
Sharp scissors
Strong thread to tie up the pom-poms
Ribbon, twine, or string to hang pom-poms (I used Habotai Silk Natural-Dyed Ribbon in Silver, ⁵⁄₈in/1.6cm wide, by Lancaster and Cornish. One 3¼yd/3m spool makes about 15 pom-poms.)

FOR THE POM-POMS
Following the instructions that come with the pom-pom maker, make a pom-pom from one of the yarns, tying it together very firmly around the center with the strong thread. Do not open the pom-pom maker yet, or trim the ends of the thread.

Cut an 8in (20cm) length of ribbon and knot the ends together. Pass an end of the thread through the ribbon loop and slide the knot around to be as close to the center of the pom-pom as possible. Knot the thread tightly again to secure the ribbon loop.

Open the pom-pom maker and trim the pom-pom to a neat(ish) round shape. It's quite tricky to trim the pom-poms very neatly, but personally I like them a little choppy to show the hand-made quality. Repeat in all the yarn colors until you have enough pom-poms to decorate your room, tree, or home.

A combination of my favorite things: chunky knits, pom-poms, ombré grays, and a flash of pink. Simple and fun to make, this delightfully tactile pillow features both texture and a play on color and tone. It offers a real sense of frivolity, and you could make it even bolder by using shades of blue or pink to make the pom-poms, or go for a truly multi-color pillow with a colorful background, too.

Ombré Pom-pom Pillow

SKILL LEVEL ● ● ●

SIZE
Approximately 16 x 16in (40 x 40cm)

YARN
Spuntaneous from Cascade Yarns (100% extra fine merino wool), 109yd (100m) to 7oz (200g)
   9oz (260g) in Cream (A)
Super Chunky yarn from Lauren Aston Designs (100% merino wool), 71yd (65m) to 3½oz (100g)
   ¾oz (20g) in Bright Pink (B)

For pom-poms
Jumbo yarn from Lauren Aston Designs (100% merino wool), 11yd (10m) to 3½oz (100g)
   ¾oz (20g) in Natural White
   ¾oz (20g) in Light Grey
   ¾oz (20g) in Mid Grey
   ¾oz (20g) In Granite

NEEDLES
Pair of US 17 (12mm) knitting needles
Large darning needle

OTHER MATERIALS AND EQUIPMENT
2in (5cm) pom-pom maker
Strong thread to tie up the pom-poms
16 x 16in (40 x 40cm) pillow pad

GAUGE (TENSION)
Approximately 7 stitches and 10 rows to 4in (10cm) over st st.

ABBREVIATIONS
See page 92.

FOR THE PILLOW
Cast on 30 sts in A.
Row 1: Knit.
Row 2: Purl.
Rows 3–78: Rep rows 1–2.
Change to B.
Row 79: Knit.
Row 80: [K1, p1] to end of row.
Row 81: [P1, k1] to end of row.
Row 82: [K1, p1] to end of row.
Row 83: Knit.
Change to A.
Row 84: Knit.
Bind (cast) off.

TO MAKE UP
Sew in loose ends (see page 105).
  Mattress stitch (see page 104) the cast-on and bound-(cast-) off ends together. Arrange the knitting so that the pink stripe is across the center back. Place the pillow pad inside the knitting and mattress stitch the side seams closed.
  Following the instructions that come with the pom-pom maker, make 15 pom-poms in a selection of the colors, using strong thread to tie them around the middle. Scatter the pom-poms around the pillow relatively evenly, with the darkest at the bottom and lightest at the top, and then stitch them on.

I really love the subtlety of this child's blanket; the soft colors keep it calming and cozy, while the pattern looks detailed and has real impact. A great thing about it is that the slip stitch uses only one color yarn at a time, so it's much easier to knit than it looks. Working the borders does require a bit of intarsia knitting using a second strand of color A, and I find it best to use both ends of the yarn rather than cutting it to length and risking cutting too much or too little.

Child's Slip-stitch Blanket

SKILL LEVEL ● ● ●

SIZE
39¼ x 27in (100 x 68.5cm)

YARN
Jumbo yarn from Lauren Aston Designs (100% merino wool), 11yd (10m) to 3½oz (100g)
   31¾oz (900g) in Natural White (A)
   21¼oz (600g) in Mint (B)

NEEDLES
Pair of US 50 (25mm) knitting needles

OTHER EQUIPMENT
Sewing needle and thread to match yarn

GAUGE (TENSION)
Approximately 3 stitches and 6 rows to 4in (10cm) over pattern.

ABBREVIATIONS
See page 92.

NOTES
When changing yarns to work the border, remember to link the yarns around each other so as not to create holes in the knitting (see page 103).
  Both ends of the ball of yarn A are used, with the end from the center of the ball referred to as A, and the yarn from the outside of the ball referred to as AA.

FOR THE BLANKET
Cast on 30 sts in A, using the end of yarn from the center of the ball.
Row 1: Knit.
Join in B.
Row 2: Purl.
Row 3: In A k2, change to B, [k1, yf, sl1] to last 2 sts, join in AA (using end of yarn from outside of ball), k2.
Row 4: In AA p2, change to B, [p1, yb, sl1 purlwise] to last 2 sts, change to A, p2.
Row 5: In A k2, [k1, yf, sl1] to last 2 sts, change to AA, k2.
Row 6: In AA p2, change to A, [p1, yb, sl1 purlwise] to last 2 sts, p2.
Rows 7–40: Rep rows 3–6, ending with a row 4.
Row 41: Purl all sts in A.
Bind (cast) off loosely.

TO MAKE UP
Sew in loose ends (see page 105).

Chunky, simple stitches have always been my favorites: there's something so tactile about a repetitive texture and this hot water bottle cover shows that off beautifully. It mixes simple seed (moss) and garter stitch, and finishes with a classic single rib. Using two colors that are tonally similar enhances the differences between the stitch patterns, and at the same time coordinates them.

The ribbed neck of this cover is so stretchy you can easily remove the bottle through it (simply fold the bottle in half once it's been emptied).

Hot Water Bottle Cover

SKILL LEVEL ● ● ●

SIZE
7 x 12½in (18.25 x 32.25cm) unstretched (fits a standard 4¼ pint/2 liter hot water bottle)

YARN
Super Chunky yarn from Lauren Aston Designs (100% merino wool), 71yd (65m) to 3½oz (100g)
  1¾oz (50g) in Lilac (A)
  1¾oz (50g) in Light Grey (B)

NEEDLES
Pair of US 17 (12mm) knitting needles
Large darning needle

GAUGE (TENSION)
Approximately 8 stitches and 13 rows to 4in (10cm) over both patterns.

ABBREVIATIONS
See page 92.

NOTES
When changing colors be sure to link the yarns around one another on the wrong side so you don't end up with gaps (see page 103).

When using two strands of yarn (as in row 15), use the other end of yarn from the center of the ball as the second strand.

When changing between the stitch patterns, be sure to keep the seed (moss) stitch pattern correct: stitches in both a row and in a column are always alternately knit and purl stitches.

FOR THE COVER
Cast on 29 sts in A.
Rows 1–12: [K1, p1] to last st, k1.
Row 13: [K1, p1] 7 times (so working 14 sts in seed/moss stitch), join in B, k1, change to A, [p1, k1] (so working 14 sts in seed/moss stitch).
These 2 rows set seed (moss) stitch patt in A, with one central stitch in garter stitch patt in B.
Row 14: In A work 13 sts in seed (moss) stitch, change to B, k3, change to A, work 13 sts in seed (moss) stitch.
Rows 15–27: Cont in patt as set, increasing central garter stitch section by 1 st at each end on every row and decreasing seed (moss) stitch sections accordingly, and working all seed (moss) sts in A and all garter sts in B.
Cut A and cont in B.
Row 28–35: Knit all sts.
WORKING THE NECK
Row 36: [K1, p1] to last st, k1.
Row 37: [P1, k1] to last st, p1.
These 2 rows set single rib patt.
Rows 38–42: Rep rows 36–37.
Bind (cast) off loosely.

TO MAKE UP
Sew in all loose ends (see page 105).

Fold the cover in half lengthwise and mattress stitch (see page 104) the bottom and side seams.

I'm really in love with this blanket, it just screams fun. The soft oyster color stops it overwhelming the room while the tonal pom-poms add color and texture. The knitting is satisfyingly speedy and the pom-poms can be made in any colors you fancy to complement your room—you could even put them round three or four edges of the blanket if you like (I'm just a fan of symmetry so went for two edges!). And the blanket is reversible, so choose the side with the texture you like best.

Pom-pom Trim Blanket

SKILL LEVEL ● ● ●

SIZE
Approximately 39¼ x 39¼in (100 x 100cm)

YARN
Giant yarn from Lauren Aston Designs (100% merino wool), 5½yd (5m) to 3½oz (100g)
  49½oz (1.4kg) in Oyster (A)
  1oz (30g) in each of Bright Pink, Oyster, Soft Peach, and Mink Blush

NEEDLES
Pair of US 70 (40mm) knitting needles or you can arm knit (see page 106)

OTHER MATERIALS AND EQUIPMENT
2¾in (7cm) pom-pom maker
Sewing needle and thread to match yarn
Strong thread to tie up the pom-poms, ideally to match yarn A

GAUGE (TENSION)
Approximately 1½ stitches and 1½ rows to 4in (10cm) over pattern.

ABBREVIATIONS
See page 92.

FOR THE BLANKET
Cast on 15 sts in A.
Row 1: Knit.
Row 2: Purl.
Rows 3–14: Rep rows 1–2.
Bind (cast) off loosely.

TO MAKE UP
Sew in loose ends (see page 105).

  Following the pom-pom maker instructions, wrap the yarn around one side of the maker and then the other, then cut the yarn down the middle of each wrap. Use the strong thread to tie the pom-pom very firmly and securely around the middle. Leave the ends of the thread long. Open the pom-pom maker and trim the pom-pom to a neat(ish) round shape. It's quite tricky to trim the pom-poms very neatly, but personally I like them a little choppy to show the hand-made quality. Make 14 pom-poms in a mixture of colors.

  Lay the blanket on a clean surface/floor and arrange the pom-poms along the sides of the blanket as you wish, spreading the colors evenly. Sew the pom-poms in place using the long ends you left when making the pom-poms.

Add color and texture with this fun pillow. A great starter project, the pillow is easy to knit yet still enables you to be creative with the mix of colors you use. I bought tassels in assorted colors and stitched them around the edges, but you could use any number of trimmings and any mix of colors. The options are endless!

Tassel-edge Pillow

SKILL LEVEL ● ○ ○

SIZE
Approximately 25 x 13in (66 x 33cm)

YARN
Big Wool from Rowan (100% wool), 87yd (80m) to 3½oz (100g)
3½oz (100g) in Prize (A)
3½oz (100g) in Ice Blue (B)

NEEDLES
Pair of US 17 (12mm) knitting needles
Large darning needle

OTHER MATERIALS AND EQUIPMENT
Sewing needle and thread to match either yarn or trim color
25 x 13in (66 x 33cm) pillow pad
90 x assorted color cotton tassels or other trim of your choice: I used tassels from Violet Earth Supplies (see page 110 for suppliers)

GAUGE (TENSION)
Approximately 7 stitches and 10 rows to 4in (10cm) over st st.

ABBREVIATIONS
See page 92.

FOR THE PILLOW
Cast on 25 sts in A.
Row 1: Knit.
Row 2: Purl.
Rows 3–60: Rep rows 1–2.
Bind (cast) off.

Make a second piece in B, following the same pattern.

TO MAKE UP
Sew in loose ends (see page 105).
  Place the two pieces wrong sides together and mattress stitch around three sides (see page 104). Put the pillow pad inside and mattress stitch the last side closed.
  Hand-sew tassels (or your chosen trim) evenly around all four edges of the pillow.

The ultimate in *hygge*, this bean bag was designed with tea-fueled rainy afternoons and cozy night-time stories in mind. Created with a simple and repetitive knitting pattern, it's easy to get the hang of it, but weighing in at around 6½lb (3kg), the work does get heavy, so remember to rest it on your lap and have regular (tea) breaks.

Chunky-knit Bean Bag

SKILL LEVEL ● ● ●

SIZE
27½in (70cm) diameter x 20in (50cm) tall

YARN
Jumbo yarn from Lauren Aston Designs (100% merino wool), 11yd (10m) to 3½oz (100g)
101oz (2.89kg) in Mink-Blush

NEEDLES
Pair of US 50 (25mm) knitting needles

OTHER EQUIPMENT
2¾yd (2.5m) of fabric in a matching or complementary color to line bean bag; I used peach-colored polycotton
Sewing needle and thread to match lining fabric
3¼yd (3m) of bean bag netting fabric
5 cubic feet (0.14 cubic meter) of polystyrene beans
Sewing machine (this is optional, the lining can be hand sewn)

GAUGE (TENSION)
Approximately 3 stitches and 4 rows to 4in (10cm) over pattern.

ABBREVIATIONS
See page 92.

FOR THE BEAN BAG
Cast on 22 sts.
Rows 1–2: [K1, p1] to end of row.
Rows 3–4: [P1, k1] to end of row.
Rows 5–76: Rep rows 1–4 (or until work measures approx 29½ x 86½in/75 x 220cm; don't worry if the measurements aren't exact, the yarn is very malleable).
Bind (cast) off evenly, leaving a tail about 3¼yd (3m) long.

TO MAKE UP
Wash the knitting and spare end of wool in cool water. Wearing rubber gloves, rub and squeeze it to help felt it a bit and become more hardwearing. Lay flat to dry.
  Once dry, fold the knitting in half lengthwise, right sides together, and sew two sides up with the tail of yarn, which should be felted enough to make it strong. Leave around 16in (40cm) of the tail free.

LINING
Cut 2 rectangles of lining fabric, each measuring 30¼ x 43¼in (77 x 110cm). Right sides together, lay one on top of the other and sew the side seams and bottom seam. At one bottom corner, pull the front and back pieces apart to create a triangle with the bottom seam running vertically through the center. Measure 4in (10cm) from the point down the vertical seam and draw a line horizontal to the seam to create a triangle.
Sew across the horizontal line and trim off the excess triangle in the corner. Repeat on the other bottom corner. This helps give the lining some shape.

If you have a sewing machine, then sew across the bottom of the bean bag netting. If not, then just knot it tightly. It's very stretchy so the shape shouldn't be a problem. Place the netting inside the lining and fill it with the polystyrene beans (be careful as they can get everywhere!).

Leaving space so the beans can move around, knot the top of the netting tightly so no beans can escape. Sew around the open top of the lining with running stitch, and pull it tight to cinch the top of the lining closed.

Pull the knitted piece over the lining, making sure the cinched top of the lining is at the same end as the opening in the knitting. Using the last 16in (40cm) of the felted wool, thread it through each stitch on the knitted opening and slowly and carefully pull it tight to cinch the top closed as tightly as possible (be careful the wool doesn't pull apart). Knot it to hold the end closed and tuck in the loose ends.

This fun and vibrant hanging plant pot holder not only helps bring a bit of nature into your home, but can also brighten up any corner. The strong color really stands out from afar, and when you get closer you notice that it's broken up by the use of different stitches. For this pattern I thought a diagonal stitch change would be a great combination with the sloping lines created by the yarn hanging strings. Both the diagonal stitch change and the shaping are easier than they look.

Hanging Plant Pot Holder

SKILL LEVEL ● ● ◉

SIZE
Approximately 4½in (11cm) deep x 4½in (11cm) internal diameter (fits a plant pot 5in (13cm) deep x 5½in (14cm) diameter)

YARN
Magnum from Cascade Yarns (100% Peruvian highland wool), 123yd (112m) to 8¾oz (250g)
2¼oz (65g) in Poinsettia

NEEDLES
Set of 4 US 17 (12mm) double-pointed knitting needles
Large darning needle

OTHER MATERIALS AND EQUIPMENT
Plain white plant pot 5in (13cm) deep x 5½in (14cm) diameter
Stitch marker

GAUGE (TENSION)
Approximately 7 stitches and 11 rows to 4in (10cm) over st st.

ABBREVIATIONS
See page 92.

NOTES
The two stitch patterns used are stockinette (stocking) stitch—where in the round every stitch is a knit—and double seed (moss) stitch—where two rounds of k1, p1 are alternated with two rounds of p1, k1.

FOR THE HOLDER
Cast on 24 sts.
Divide the sts equally between 3 needles and making sure the cast-on is not twisted, join it into a circle and place the stitch marker to mark the beginning of the round.
Round 1: Purl.
Round 2: Knit.
Round 3: Purl.
Now start the diagonal pattern. Although there are 24 stitches, each round will work 25 stitches to move the pattern round 1 stitch at a time. I find it easier to place a stitch marker at the end of the round and then move it round 1 stitch at a time so you can see which stitch you finished on in the last round and move on by 1.
Round 4: K13, [p1, k1] 6 times, place marker.
Rounds 5–6: K13, [k1, p1] 6 times, move marker 1 stitch forward.
Rounds 7–8: K13, [p1, k1] 6 times, move marker 1 stitch forward.
Rounds 9–16: Rep rounds 5–8.
Round 17: [K2tog] to end of row. *(12 sts)*
Round 18: Knit.
Round 19: [K2tog] to end of row. *(6 sts)*
Cut yarn and thread through rem 6 sts, and pull up and secure tightly to close hole.

TO MAKE UP
Sew in loose ends (see page 105).
Cut 3 strands of yarn each approximately 2yd (2m) long.
At three evenly spaced intervals around the rim of the holder, thread one end of each strand through. Pull all the ends up and to the center so they hold the pot evenly. Knot at the top (or further down depending on your desired hanging height), leaving a loop to hang the holder from.

Introduce some texture and color into your home with this diagonal contrast stitch pillow, finished with a classic blanket stitch. This is a good pattern for anyone who is a beginner to color knitting, as it uses only simple knit and purl stitches but the color and stitch combination alters on each side, giving it subtle interest and definition. If you haven't used the intarsia knitting technique before you can find instructions on page 103.

Diagonal Stitch Pillow

SKILL LEVEL ● ● ○

SIZE
16 x 16in (40 x 40cm)

YARN
Spuntaneous from Cascade Yarns (100% extra fine merino wool), 109yd (100m) 7oz (200g)
    5oz (140g) Silver (A)
    5oz (140g) Blue Coral (B)
    ¾oz (20g) Cream (C)

NEEDLES
Pair of US 17 (12mm) knitting needles
Large darning needle

OTHER MATERIALS
16 x 16in (40 x 40cm) pillow pad

GAUGE (TENSION)
Approximately 6½ stitches and 10 rows to 4in (10cm) over pattern.

ABBREVIATIONS
See page 92.

NOTES
When changing colors, remember to link the yarns around each other so as to prevent holes from appearing (see page 103).

FOR THE PILLOW

PANEL 1
Cast on 26 sts in A.
Row 1: Knit.
Row 2: Purl.
Rows 3–13: Rep rows 1–2, finishing with a row 1.
Join in B.
Row 14: In B k1, change to A and purl to end of row.
Row 15: In A k24, change to D, k2.
Row 16: In B k3, change to A and purl to end of row.
Row 17: In A k22, change to D, k4.
Cont in patt as set, working all A sts in stockinette (stocking) stitch (knit 1 row, purl 1 row), and all B sts in garter st (knit every row), and AT THE SAME TIME increasing the number of sts in B by 1 on every row.
Row 38: In B k25, change to A, p1.
Break A and cont in B.
Rows 39–45: Knit in B.
Bind (cast) off.

PANEL 2
Work as for Side 1, but swap colors A and B.

TO MAKE UP
Sew in loose ends (see page 105).
    Place both panels around the pillow pad so that A on panel 1 is touching A on panel 2 (the sides wont align but the top and bottom of both panels should run into the same color on the other side).
    Using C, blanket stitch (see page 105) the panels together around all four edges.

This runner is all about the impact. The subtle color change is gradual, but over all it makes a real statement. The runner is easy enough to make and super-quick due to the huge scale. Personally, I think that when the finished piece has so much impact, it's best to use neutral colors, as it doesn't need to be any "louder."

Ombré Giant-knit Bedrunner

SKILL LEVEL ● ● ○

SIZE
Approximately 52¾ x 20in (134 x 50cm)

YARN
Giant yarn from Lauren Aston Designs (100% merino wool), 5½yd (5m) to 3½oz (100g)
  23oz (650g) in Granite (A)
  23oz (650g) in Mid Grey (B)
  23oz (650g) Light Grey (C)

NEEDLES
Pair of US 70 (40mm) knitting needles or you can arm knit

OTHER EQUIPMENT
Sewing needle and thread to match yarn

GAUGE (TENSION)
Approximately 1½ stitches and 2 rows to 4in (10cm) over st st.

ABBREVIATIONS
See page 92.

NOTES
On the rows where you use two colors, try to twist them together as much as possible; not only will this help blend them together but it will also prevent the stitches from being too bulky.
If you are arm-knitting, then knit all the rows (see page 106), mixing colors as instructed in the pattern.

FOR THE BEDRUNNER
Cast on 20 sts in A.
Row 1: Knit.
Row 2: Purl.
Join in B and use A and B held together.
Row 3: Knit.
Cut A and cont in B only.
Row 4: Purl.
Row 5: Knit.
Row 6: Purl.
Join in C and use B and C held together.
Row 7: Knit.
Cut B and cont in C only.
Row 8: Purl.
Row 9: Knit.
Row 10: Purl.
Bind (cast) off loosely.

TO MAKE UP
Sew in loose ends (see page 105).

This fun and fluffy pom-pom garland can be made in any colors and to any length. You could easily make a loop at each end and hang it horizontally like a bunting, and if you have enough shades of one color, you could make an ombré version.

Pom-pom Garland

SKILL LEVEL ● ● ●

SIZE
Approximately 1yd (1m) long

YARN
Jumbo yarn from Lauren Aston Designs (100% merino wool), 11yd (10m) to 3½oz (100g)
OR
Giant yarn from Lauren Aston Designs (100% merino wool), 5½yd (5m) to 3½oz (100g)

   $^3/_8$ oz (10g) each of Oyster, Soft Peach, Mink Blush, Pewter Brown, Damson, Shadow, Lilac, Light Grey, Mid Grey, Granite, and Bright Pink

OTHER MATERIALS AND EQUIPMENT
2¾in (7cm) pom-pom maker
Sharp scissors
Strong thread to tie up the pom-poms
Ribbon, twine, or string (I used pink twine)
Embroidery needle

FOR THE GARLAND
You need to make one pom-pom in each color.
   Following the pom-pom maker instructions, wrap the yarn around one side of the maker and then the other, then cut the yarn down the middle of each wrap. Use the strong thread to tie the pom-pom very firmly and securely around the middle. Open the pom-pom maker and trim the pom-pom to a neat(ish) round shape. It's quite tricky to trim the pom-poms very neatly, but personally I like them a little choppy to show the hand-made quality.

TO MAKE UP
Once all your pom-poms are made up, using an embroidery needle threaded with a long piece of ribbon, twine, or string, push the needle through the center of each pom-pom, one at a time, in the order you'd like them to hang.
   Leave about 8–13in (20–30cm) of bare twine at one end (or both ends if you'd like). To make a hanging loop, simply double the bare twine back on itself and knot it tightly at the base of the first/last pom-pom. Push the pom-pom up a little so it covers the knot as much as possible, and adjust the pom-poms on the twine so that they are evenly spaced.

I wanted to make something compact and colorful using this stitch pattern, so I opted for a lap blanket that's perfect for snuggling up on the couch. It can also easily be made in a larger size if you'd prefer it to go at the end of the bed, or to cover more than one person. You can follow the same pattern, but cast on either 24 or 30 stitches to make it 63in (160cm) or 79in (200cm) wide—depending on the width of the bed and how much you'd like it to hang over the sides—then just knit the pattern until you reach the desired length.

Basketweave Lap Blanket

SKILL LEVEL ● ● ○

SIZE
Approximately 31½ x 31½in (80 x 80cm)

YARN
Giant yarn from Lauren Aston Designs (100% merino wool), 5½yd (5m) to 3½oz (100g)
   46oz (1.3kg) in Baby Blue

NEEDLES
Pair of US 70 (40mm) knitting needles

OTHER EQUIPMENT
Sewing needle and thread to match yarn

GAUGE (TENSION)
Approximately 1½ stitches and 2 rows to 4in (10cm) over pattern.

ABBREVIATIONS
See page 92.

FOR THE BLANKET
Cast on 12 sts.
Rows 1 and 3: [K3, p3] to end of row.
Rows 2 and 4: [P3, k3] to end of row.
Rows 5 and 7: [P3, k3] to end of row.
Rows 6 and 8: [K3, p3] to end of row.
Rows 9–16: Rep rows 1–8.
Bind (cast) off loosely.

TO MAKE UP
Sew in loose ends (see page 105).

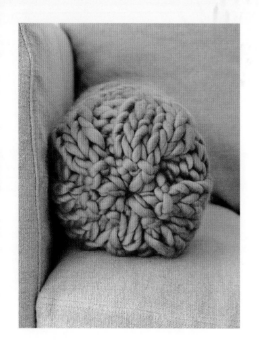

This traditional bolster pillow is brought bang up to date by mixing classic cabling and stylish chunky knit. It adds texture and color to your room, creating a staple home accessory that can sit on a chair, sofa, or bed all year round. The shaped cables look more complicated to knit than they really are, and the large yarn makes it easy to see where your stitches are.

Cable-knit Bolster Pillow

SKILL LEVEL ● ● ●

SIZE
22in (55cm) long x 7in (18cm) diameter

YARN
Fat Bubba from Melanie Porter (100% merino wool), 82yd (75m) to 17½oz (500g) 15½oz (440g) in Moss

NEEDLES
Pair of US 50 (25mm) knitting needles
US 50 (25mm) cable needle or double-pointed knitting needle
Large darning needle

OTHER MATERIALS
16 x 6in (40 x 15cm) bolster pillow pad

GAUGE (TENSION)
Approximately 5 stitches and 6 rows to 4in (10cm) over pattern.

ABBREVIATIONS
Cr3L: slip next 2 sts onto cable needle and hold at front of work, p1 from left-hand needle, k2 from cable needle.
Cr3R: slip next st onto cable needle and hold at back of work, k2 from left-hand needle, p1 from cable needle.
See ALSO page 92.

FOR THE PILLOW
Cast on 25 sts, leaving a tail of yarn approx 4in (10cm) long.
Row 1 (RS): P2, k4, p2, k9, p2, k4, p2.
Row 2 and every other WS row: Knit all knit stitches and purl all purl stitches.
Rows 3 and 5: As row 1.
Row 7: P2, C4B, p2, Cr3L, Cr3R, Cr3L, p2, C4F, p2.
Row 9: P2, k4, p3, C4B, p2, k2, p2, k4, p2.
Row 11: P2, C4B, p2, Cr3R, Cr3L, Cr3R, p2, C4F, p2.
Row 13: P2, k4, p2, k2, p2, C4F, p3, k4, p2.
Rows 15–30: Rep rows 7–14.
Rows 31–34: Knit all knit stitches and purl all purl stitches.
Bind (cast) off leaving a tail of yarn approx. 4in (10cm) long.

TO MAKE UP
Thread the yarn tails left at each end of the knitting through the row of cast-on/bound- (cast-) off stitches and pull tight to cinch the hole closed. Secure the ends on the WS.
Fit the knitting over the pillow pad and mattress stitch (see page 104) the seam.

If you're after impact, this giant knit blanket is the one. With its dramatic cable through the center and knit in such a bold and modern color, it makes a huge and cozy statement. It's a little awkward to knit as you are using three large needles, but thankfully as the yarn is so thick, it doesn't take much time to make, so it's not a long struggle, and will definitely be worth the effort in the end.

Giant Cable Blanket

SKILL LEVEL ● ● ●

SIZE
65 x 31½in (166 x 80cm)

YARN
Giant yarn from Lauren Aston Designs (100% merino wool), 5½yd (5m) to 3½oz (100g)
116½oz (3.3kg) in Mustard

NEEDLES
Pair of US 70 (40mm) knitting needles
US 70 (40mm) cable needle or double-pointed knitting needle

OTHER EQUIPMENT
Sewing needle and thread to match yarn

GAUGE (TENSION)
Approximately 1½ stitches and 2½ rows to 4in (10cm) over pattern.

ABBREVIATIONS
Cr3L: slip next 2 sts onto cable needle and hold at front of work, p1 from left-hand needle, k2 from cable needle.
Cr3R: slip next st onto cable needle and hold at back of work, k2 from left-hand needle, p1 from cable needle.
See ALSO page 92.

FOR THE BLANKET
Cast on 25 sts.
Row 1 (RS): P2, k4, p2, k9, p2, k4, p2.
Row 2 and every other WS row: Knit all knit stitches and purl all purl stitches.
Row 3: P2, C4B, p2, Cr3L, Cr3R, Cr3L, p2, C4F, p2.
Row 5: P2, k4, p3, C4B, p2, k2, p2, k4, p2.
Row 7: P2, C4B, p2, Cr3R, Cr3L, Cr3R, p2, C4F, p2.
Row 9: P2, k4, p2, k2, p2, C4F, p3, k4, p2.
Row 10: K2, p4, k3, p4, k2, p2, k2, p4, k2.
Row 11–18: Rep rows 3–10.
Bind (cast) off loosely.

TO MAKE UP
Sew in loose ends (see page 105).

CHAPTER THREE

Techniques

On the following pages you'll find the basic techniques that you will need to knit the patterns in this book. Most of the projects use only simple techniques, so a novice knitter can confidently tackle them. If a pattern does include a technique that is new to you, then I suggest practicing it with some scrap yarn before you start the project.

The knitting needles, yarn, and any other items that you will need are listed at the beginning of each pattern. You can substitute the yarn recommended in a pattern with the same weight of yarn in a different brand, but you will need to check the gauge (tension) (see page 96) to make sure that the substitute yarn knits up to the same number of stitches per inch (centimeter). When calculating the quantity of substitute yarn you will need, it is the length of yarn in each ball that you need to check, rather than the weight of the ball; the length of yarn in each ball of the recommended project yarn is given in the materials list for that pattern.

Holding needles

If you are a knitting novice, you will need to discover which is the most comfortable way for you to hold your needles. You may find the very thick needles used in some projects a bit difficult to handle at first, but you will become familiar with them through use, and the knitting does grow so quickly!

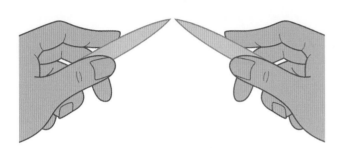

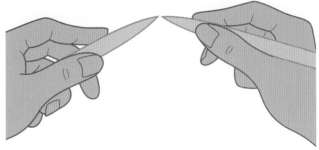

LIKE A KNIFE

Pick up the needles, one in each hand, as if you were holding a knife and fork—that is to say, with your hands lightly over the top of each needle. As you knit, you will tuck the blunt end of the right-hand needle under your arm, let go with your hand, and use your hand to manipulate the yarn, returning your hand to the needle to move the stitches along.

LIKE A PEN

Now try changing the right hand so you are holding the needle as you would hold a pen, with your thumb and forefinger lightly gripping the needle close to its pointed tip and the shaft resting in the crook of your thumb. As you knit, you will not need to let go of the needle but simply slide your right hand forward to manipulate the yarn.

Holding yarn

As you knit, you will be working stitches off the left-hand needle and onto the right-hand needle, and the yarn you are working with needs to be tensioned and manipulated to produce an even fabric. To hold and tension the yarn you can use either your right or left hand, depending on the method you are going to use to make the stitches.

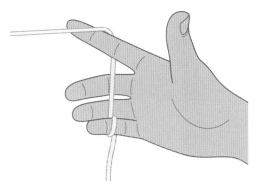

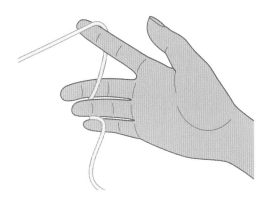

YARN IN RIGHT HAND

To knit and purl in the US/UK style (see pages 94 and 95), hold the yarn in your right hand. You can wind the yarn around your fingers in different ways, depending on how tightly you need to hold it to achieve an even gauge (tension). Try both ways shown to find out which works best for you.

To hold the yarn tightly (left), wind it right around your little finger, under your ring and middle fingers, then pass it over your index finger, which will manipulate the yarn. For a looser hold (right), catch the yarn between your little and ring fingers, pass it under your middle finger, then over your index finger.

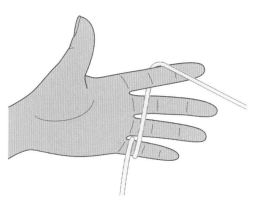

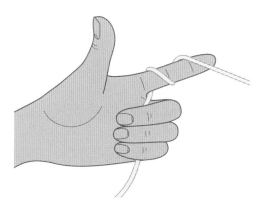

YARN IN LEFT HAND

To knit and purl in the Continental style (see pages 94 and 95), hold the yarn in your left hand. This method is sometimes easier for left-handed people to use, though many left-handers are quite comfortable knitting with the yarn in their right hand. Try the ways shown to find out which works best for you.

To hold the yarn tightly (left), wind it right around your little finger, under your ring and middle fingers, then pass it over your index finger, which will manipulate the yarn. For a looser hold (right), fold your little, ring, and middle fingers over the yarn, and wind it twice around your index finger.

Abbreviations

A, B, C	yarn colors as listed in materials		**oz**	ounce(s)
approx	approximately		**p**	purl
beg	begin(s)(ning)		**p2tog**	purl two stitches together
C4B	cable four stitches (or number stated) back		**patt(s)**	pattern(s)
C4F	cable four stitches (or number stated) front		**rem**	remain(ing)
cm	centimeter(s)		**rep**	repeat
cont	continue		**RS**	right side
Cr3L	cross three stitches left (front): slip next 2 sts onto cable needle and hold at front of work, p1 from left-hand needle, k2 from cable needle		**sl**	slip
			ssk	slip one stitch, slip one stitch, knit slipped stitches together
Cr3R	cross three stitches right (back): slip next st onto cable needle and hold at back of work, k2 from left-hand needle, p1 from cable needle		**st st**	stockinette (stocking) stitch
			st(s)	stitch(es)
			tog	together
DK	double knit		**WS**	wrong side
foll(s)	follow(s)(ing)		**yb**	yarn back
g(r)	gram		**yf**	yarn front
in(s)	inch; inches		**yo**	yarn over needle
inc	increase(s)(ing)		**[ ]**	work instructions within brackets as many times as stated
k	knit			
k2tog	knit two stitches together		*****	work instructions following/between asterisks as many times as stated
m	meters			
mm	millimeters			

Making a slip knot

You will need to make a slip knot to form your first cast-on stitch.

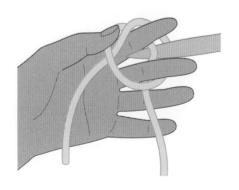

1 With the ball of yarn on your right, lay the end of the yarn on the palm of your left hand and hold it in place with your left thumb. With your right hand, take the yarn around your top two fingers to form a loop. Take the knitting needle through the back of the loop from right to left and use it to pick up the strand nearest to the yarn ball, as shown in the diagram. Pull the strand through to form a loop at the front.

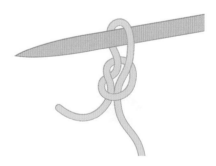

2 Slip the yarn off your fingers, leaving the loop on the needle. Gently pull on both yarn ends to tighten the knot. Then pull on the yarn leading to the ball of yarn to tighten the knot on the needle.

Casting on

This is the process of creating the first row of stitches on the needle.

CABLE CAST ON

This method uses two needles and produces a firm edge that matches in well with the stitch pattern of stockinette (stocking) stitch.

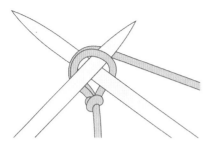 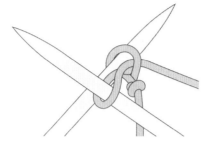 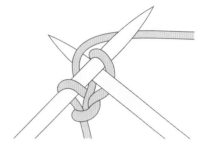

1 Make a slip knot (see page 92). Put the needle with the slip knot into your left hand. Insert the point of the other needle into the front of the slip knot and under the left-hand needle. Wind the yarn from the ball of yarn around the tip of the right-hand needle.

2 Using the tip of the needle, draw the yarn through the slip knot to form a loop. This loop is the new stitch. Slip the loop from the right-hand needle onto the left-hand needle.

3 *To make the next stitch, insert the tip of the right-hand needle between the two stitches. Wind the yarn over the right-hand needle, from left to right, then draw the yarn through to form a loop. Transfer this loop to the left-hand needle. Repeat from * until you have cast on the right number of stitches for the project.

THUMB CAST ON

This method creates a slightly stretchy cast on row that matches in well with garter stitch and rib. Because you are working with the tail end (the cut end) of the yarn as well as the ball end, you need to estimate the length of yarn needed to cast on all the stitches required. Cast on 10 stitches, then take them off and measure the length of yarn you needed to make them. Divide that length by 10, then multiply by the number of stitches you need. Add on 6in (15cm) (or the amount stated in the project) for the tail left at the end of the cast-on row.

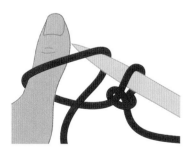 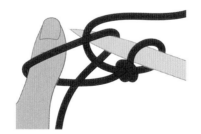 

1 Measure out the required length of yarn and make a slip knot (see page 92) at that point. Hold the knitting needle in your right hand. *From front to back, wrap the tail end of the yarn around your left thumb.

2 Using your right hand, slip the point of the knitting needle under the yarn wrapped around your thumb, as shown. Wrap the ball end of the yarn around the point of the needle.

3 Pull the needle, and the yarn around it, through the loop around your thumb. Slip your left thumb out of the loop. Pull gently on the tail end of the yarn to tighten the stitch. Repeat from * until you have cast on the right number of stitches for the project.

Knit stitch

There are only two stitches to master in knitting; knit stitch and purl stitch. Most people in the English-speaking world knit using a method called English (or American) knitting. However, in parts of Europe, people prefer a method known as Continental knitting.

US/UK STYLE

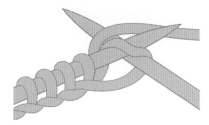

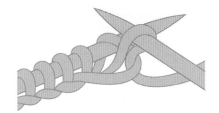

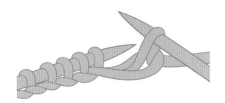

1 Hold the needle with the cast-on stitches in your left hand, and then insert the point of the right-hand needle into the front of the first stitch from left to right. Wind the yarn around the point of the right-hand needle, from left to right.

2 With the tip of the right-hand needle, pull the yarn through the stitch to form a loop. This loop is the new stitch.

3 Slip the original stitch off the left-hand needle by gently pulling the right-hand needle to the right. Repeat these steps till you have knitted all the stitches on the left-hand needle. To work the next row, transfer the needle with all the stitches into your left hand.

CONTINENTAL STYLE

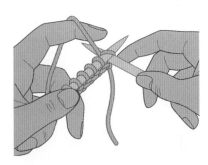

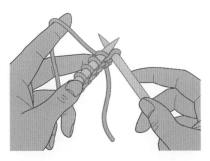

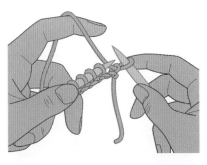

1 Hold the needle with the stitches to be knitted in your left hand, and then insert the tip of the right-hand needle into the front of the first stitch from left to right. Holding the yarn fairly taut with your left hand at the back of your work, use the tip of the right-hand needle to pick up a loop of yarn.

2 With the tip of the right-hand needle, bring the yarn through the original stitch to form a loop. This loop is the new stitch.

3 Slip the original stitch off the left-hand needle by gently pulling the right-hand needle to the right. Repeat these steps till you have knitted all the stitches on the left-hand needle. To work the next row, transfer the needle with all the stitches into your left hand.

Purl stitch

As with knit stitch, purl stitch can be formed in two ways. If you are new to knitting, try both techniques to see which works better for you: left-handed people may find the Continental method easier to master.

US/UK STYLE

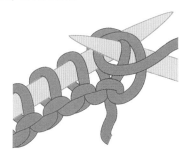  

1 Hold the needle with the stitches in your left hand, and then insert the point of the right-hand needle into the front of the first stitch from right to left. Wind the yarn around the point of the right-hand needle, from right to left.

2 With the tip of the right-hand needle, pull the yarn through the stitch to form a loop. This loop is the new stitch.

3 Slip the original stitch off the left-hand needle by gently pulling the right-hand needle to the right. Repeat these steps till you have purled all the stitches on the left-hand needle. To work the next row, transfer the needle with all the stitches into your left hand.

CONTINENTAL STYLE

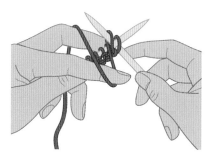  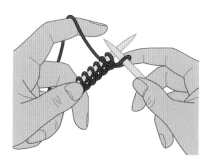

1 Hold the needle with the stitches to be knitted in your left hand, and then insert the tip of the right-hand needle into the front of the first stitch from right to left. Holding the yarn fairly taut at the front of the work, move the tip of the right-hand needle under the working yarn, then push your left index finger downward, as shown, to hold the yarn around the needle.

2 With the tip of the right-hand needle, bring the yarn through the original stitch to form a loop.

3 Slip the original stitch off the left-hand needle by gently pulling the right-hand needle to the right. Repeat these steps till you have purled all the stitches on the left-hand needle. To work the next row, transfer the needle with all the stitches into your left hand.

Binding (casting) off

You need to bind (cast) off the stitches to complete the projects and stop the knitting unraveling.

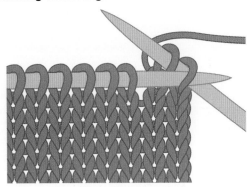 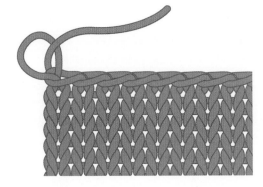

1 First knit two stitches in the normal way. With the point of the left-hand needle, pick up the first stitch you have just knitted and lift it over the second stitch. Knit another stitch so that there are two stitches on the right-hand needle again. Repeat the process of lifting the first stitch over the second stitch. Continue this process until there is just one stitch remaining on the right-hand needle.

2 Break the yarn, leaving a tail of yarn long enough to sew the work together (see page 104). Pull the tail all the way through the last stitch. Slip the stitch off the needle and pull it fairly tightly to make sure it is secure.

Gauge (tension)

A gauge (tension) is given with each pattern to help you make your item the same size as the sample. The gauge (tension) is given as the number of stitches and rows in a 4-in (10-cm) square of knitting.

Using the recommended yarn and needles, cast on 8 stitches more than the gauge (tension) instruction asks for—so if you need to have 10 stitches to 4in (10cm), cast on 18 stitches. Working in pattern as instructed, work 8 rows more than is needed. Bind (cast) off loosely.

Lay the swatch flat without stretching it. Lay a ruler across the stitches as shown, with the 2in (5cm) mark centered on the knitting, then put a pin in the knitting at the start of the ruler and at the 4in (10cm) mark: the pins should be well away from the edges of the swatch. Count the number of stitches between the pins. Repeat the process across the rows to count the number of rows to 4in (10cm). On projects such as blankets, a precise gauge (tension) is not vital.

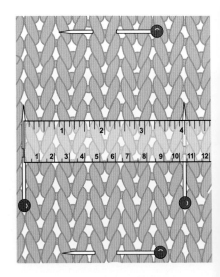

If the number of stitches and rows you've counted is the same as the number asked for in the instructions, you have the correct gauge (tension). If you do not have the same number then you will need to change your gauge (tension).

To change gauge (tension) you should not try to simply knit more tightly or loosely: all knitters have a "natural" gauge (tension) depending on their personal knitting style, and trying to change that usually just results in uneven knitting. Instead, you need to change the size of your knitting needles. A good rule of thumb to follow is that one difference in needle size will create a difference of one stitch in the gauge (tension). You will need to use larger needles to achieve fewer stitches and smaller ones to achieve more stitches.

Knitting in the round

You can knit seamless tubes by working round and round rather than back and forth. There are two ways of doing this, depending on how large the tube needs to be. When you work in the round you only work knit stitches (see page 94) to produce stockinette (stocking) stitch.

CIRCULAR NEEDLE

These needles have short straight tips that are joined with a nylon cable. As well as the usual needle size information, the pattern will tell you what length of needle you need so that your stitches fit on it without stretching.

1 Cast on the number of stitches needed (see page 93); just ignore the cable connecting the two tips and cast on the stitches as if you were using two separate needles. Spread out the cast-on row along the length of the cable and make sure that it is not twisted or you will end up with a twist in the knitting.

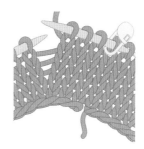

2 Simply knit the stitches from the right-hand tip onto the left-hand tip, sliding them around the cable as you work. The first stitch is the beginning of the round, so place a round marker on the needle to keep track of the rounds. When you get back to the marker, you have completed one round. Just slip the marker onto the right-hand tip of the needle and knit the next round.

DOUBLE-POINTED NEEDLES

If you do not have enough stitches to stretch around a circular needle, then you need to work on double-pointed needles. This is one of those knitting techniques that looks terrifying, but isn't actually that hard to do; you just ignore all the needles other than the two you are working with. Double-pointed needles—often called "dpns"—come in sets of four or five and a pattern will tell you how many you need.

1 Divide evenly into three (if using four needles), or into four (if using five needles), the number of stitches you need to cast on. Here, a set of four needles is being used. Cast on (see page 93) to one needle one-third of the number of stitches needed, plus one extra stitch. Slip the extra stitch onto the second needle. Repeat the process, not forgetting to count the extra stitch, until the right number of stitches is cast on to each of the needles.

2 Arrange the needles in a triangle with the tips overlapping as shown here. As with circular knitting, make sure that the cast-on edge is not twisted and place a round marker to keep track of the rounds. Pull the working tail of yarn across from the last stitch and using the free needle, knit the first stitch off the first needle (see page 94), knitting it firmly and pulling the yarn tight. Knit the rest of the stitches on the first needle, which then becomes the free one, ready to knit the stitches off the second needle. Knit the stitches off each needle in turn; when you get back to the marker, you have completed one round. Slip the marker onto the next needle and knit the next round.

Increasing

A very simple method of increasing is used in projects in this book.

INCREASE ON A KNIT ROW (INC)

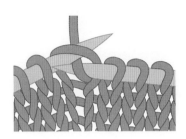 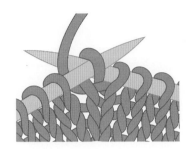 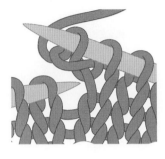

1 Knit the next stitch on the left-hand needle in the usual way (see page 94), but do not slip the "old" stitch off the left-hand needle.

2 Move the right-hand needle behind the left-hand needle and put it into the same stitch again, but through the back of the stitch this time. Knit the stitch again.

3 Now slip the "old" stitch off the left-hand needle in the usual way.

Decreasing

There are three different ways of decreasing used in this book, but they are all easy to work.

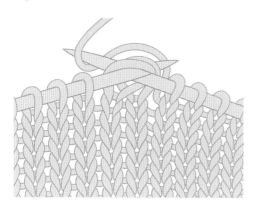

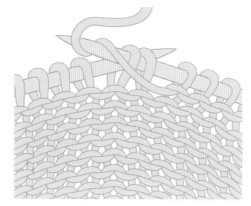

KNIT TWO TOGETHER (K2TOG)

This is the simplest way of decreasing. Simply insert the right-hand needle through two stitches instead of the normal one, and then knit them in the usual way (see page 94). The same principle is used to knit three stitches together; just insert the right-hand needle through three instead of through two.

PURL TWO TOGETHER (P2TOG)

To make a simple decrease on a purl row, insert the right-hand needle through two stitches instead of the normal one, and then purl them in the usual way (see page 95).

SLIP, SLIP, KNIT (SSK)

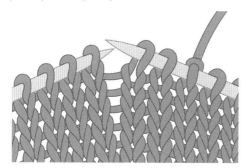

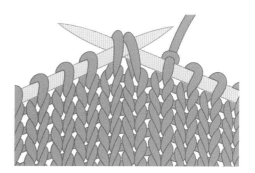

1 Slip one stitch knitwise (see page 100), and then the next stitch knitwise onto the right-hand needle, without knitting either of them.

2 Insert the left-hand needle from left to right through the front loops of both the slipped stitches and knit them in the usual way (see page 94).

Slipping stitches

This means moving stitches from one needle to the other without knitting or purling them. They can be slipped knitwise or purlwise depending on the row you are working, or any specific pattern instructions.

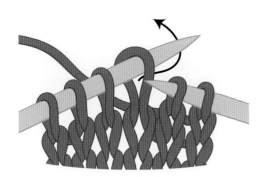

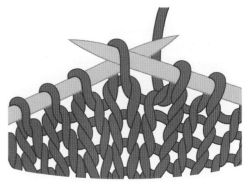

KNITWISE
From left to right, put the right-hand needle into the next stitch on the left-hand needle (as shown by the arrow) and slip it across onto the right-hand needle without working it.

PURLWISE
You can slip a stitch purlwise on a purl row or a knit row. From right to left, put the right-hand needle into the next stitch on the left-hand needle and slip it across onto the right-hand needle without working it.

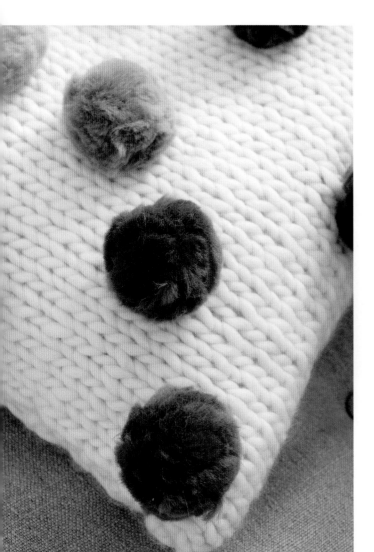

Yarnover (yo)

To make a yarnover, you wind the yarn around the right-hand needle to make an extra loop that is worked as a stitch on the next row.

Bring the yarn between the tips of the needles to the front. Take the yarn over the right-hand needle to the back and knit the next stitch on the left-hand needle (see page 94). Be sure not to confuse "yo" with the abbreviations "yf" or "yb," both of which are used in this book (see page 92 for explanations of these terms).

Cables

This is another technique that looks difficult, but really isn't. All you are doing is moving groups of stitches using a cable needle. The principle is the same no matter how many stitches are being moved, and is shown here as a six-stitch cable. To work a four-stitch cable, slip two stitches onto the needle and knit two, rather than three.

CABLE SIX FRONT (C6F)
This cable twists to the left.

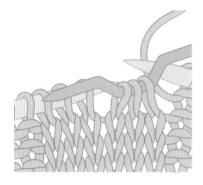

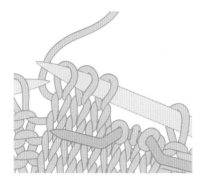

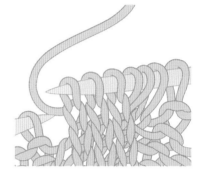

1 Work to the position of the cable. Slip the next three stitches on the left-hand needle purlwise (see page 100) onto the cable needle, then leave the cable needle in front of the work.

2 Knit the next three stitches off the left-hand needle in the usual way (see page 94).

3 Then knit the three stitches off the cable needle. The cable is completed.

CABLE SIX BACK (C6B)
This cable twists to the right.

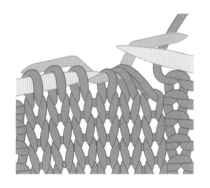

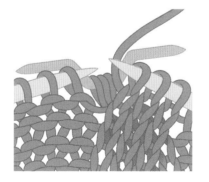

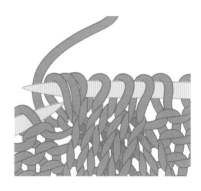

1 Work to the position of the cable. Slip the next three stitches on the left-hand needle purlwise (see page 100) onto the cable needle, then leave the cable needle at the back of the work.

2 Knit the next three stitches off the left-hand needle in the usual way (see page 94).

3 Then knit the three stitches off the cable needle. The cable is completed.

Picking up stitches

For some projects, you will need to pick up stitches along either a horizontal edge (the cast-on or bound-/cast-off edge of your knitting), or a vertical edge (the edges of your rows of knitting).

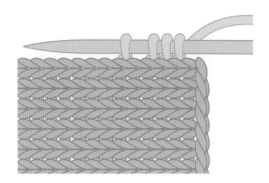

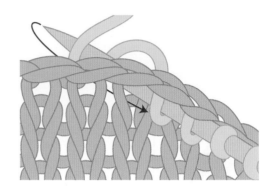

ALONG A ROW-END EDGE

With the right side of the knitting facing you, insert a knitting needle from the front to back between the first and second stitches of the first row. Wind the yarn around the needle and pull through a loop to form the new stitch. Normally you have more gaps between rows than stitches you need to pick up and knit. To make sure your picking up is even, you will have to miss a gap every few rows.

ALONG A CAST-ON OR BOUND- (CAST-) OFF EDGE

This is worked in the same way as picking up stitches along a vertical edge, except that you will work through the cast-on stitches rather than the gaps between rows. You will normally have the same number of stitches to pick up and knit as there are existing stitches.

Knitting in different colors

Only the intarsia color knitting technique is used in this book. This involves having separate balls of yarn for each area and twisting the yarns together where you change from one color to another. It's important to change yarn colors in the right way when you are working, to keep the knitted fabric flat and smooth and to prevent any holes or gaps appearing.

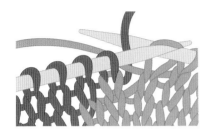
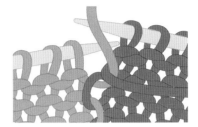
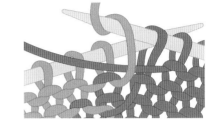

ON THE RIGHT SIDE

When you want to change colors and the color change is vertical or sloping to the right, take the first color over the second color. Then pick up the second color, so the strands of yarn cross each other.

ON THE WRONG SIDE

On this side it is easy to see how the yarns must be interlinked at each color change.

This is worked in almost the same way as on the right side. When you want to change colors and the color change is vertical or sloping to the left, take the first color over the second color. Then pick up the second color, so the strands of yarn cross each other.

Crochet chain

The Chevron-edge Clutch Purse (see page 22) requires a simple crochet chain, which can be made either using a hook, as shown here, of by using your fingers to pull the loops of yarn through each other.

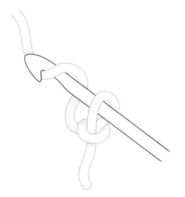
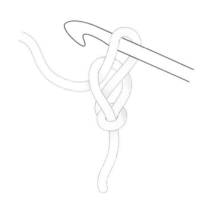

1 Make a slip knot on the crochet hook in the same way as for knitting (see page 92). Holding the slip stitch on the hook, wind the yarn around the hook from the back to the front, then catch the yarn in the crochet-hook tip.

2 Pull the yarn through the slip stitch on the crochet hook to make the second link in the chain. Continue in this way till the chain is the length needed.

Sewing seams

There are various sewing-up stitches, and the patterns advise you on which method to use.

MATTRESS STITCH ON ROW-END EDGES

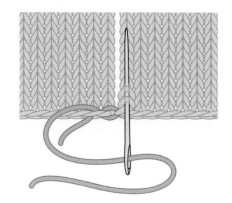

1 Right-sides up, lay the edges to be joined side by side. Thread a yarn sewing needle and from the back, bring it up between the first and second stitches of the left-hand piece, immediately above the cast-on edge. Take it across to the right-hand piece, and from the back bring it through between the first two stitches, immediately above the cast-on edge. Take it back to the left-hand piece and from the back, bring it through where it first came out. Pull the yarn through and this figure-eight will hold the cast-on edges level. Take the needle across to the right-hand piece and, from the front, take it under the bars of yarn between the first and second stitches on the next two rows up.

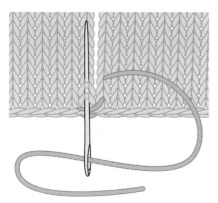

2 Take the needle across to the left-hand piece and, from the front, take it under the bars of yarn between the first and second stitches on the next two rows up. Continue in this way, taking the needle under two bars on one piece and then the other, to sew up the seam.

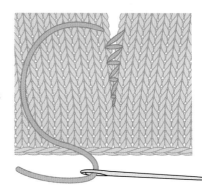

3 When you have sewn about 1in (2.5cm), gently and evenly pull the stitches tight to close the seam, and then continue to complete the sewing.

MATTRESS STITCH ON CAST-ON AND BOUND- (CAST-) OFF EDGES

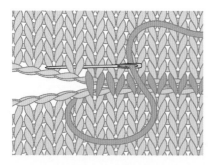

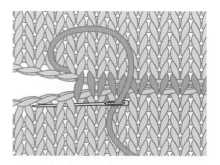

1 Right-sides up, lay the two edges to be joined side by side. Thread a yarn sewing needle with a tail left after binding (casting) off, or a long length of yarn. Secure the yarn on the back of the lower knitted piece, then bring the needle up through the middle of the first whole stitch in that piece. Take the needle under both "legs" of the first whole stitch on the upper piece, so that it comes to the front between the first and second stitches.

2 Go back into the lower piece and take the needle through to the back where it first came out, and then bring it back to the front in the middle of the next stitch along. Pull the yarn through. Take the needle under both "legs" of the next whole stitch on the upper piece. Repeat this step to sew the seam. Pull the stitches gently taut to close the seam as you work.

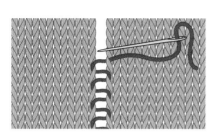

FLAT STITCH

This stitch creates a join that is completely flat. Right-sides up, lay the two edges to be joined side by side. Thread a yarn sewing needle with a tail left after binding (casting) off, or a long length of yarn. Pick up the very outermost strand of knitting from one piece and then the same strand on the other piece. Work your way along the seam, pulling the yarn up firmly every few stitches to close the seam.

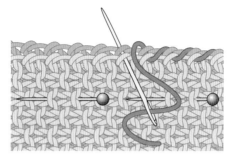

OVERSEWING

This stitch can be worked with the right or the wrong sides of the work together. Thread a yarn sewing needle with a tail left after binding (casting) off, or a long length of yarn. Bring the yarn from the back of the work, over the edge of the knitting, and out through to the back again a short distance further on.

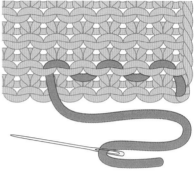

SEWING IN ENDS

The easiest way to finish yarn ends is to run a few small stitches forward then backward through your work, ideally in a seam. It is a good idea to use a yarn sewing needle to do this and take the tail between the strands that make up your yarn, as this will help make sure the end stays in place. If you are working with very thick yarn, such as Lauren Aston Designs Jumbo or Giant yarn, then use your fingers to weave the yarn tail in and out of a few stitches along the edge of the knitting. Then sew the tail neatly and firmly in place using a sewing needle and sewing thread that matches the yarn color.

BLANKET STITCH

This is a decorative way of joining two pieces of knitting together along the edges. Place the two pieces of knitting wrong sides together, matching the edges. *Insert the needle through both layers at the top of the stitch, then take it over the edge of the knitting. Pull the yarn through, making sure that the working loop goes under the needle. Repeat from *.

Arm knitting

The Twisted Stitch Arm-knit Blanket (see page 50) is made using this fun technique, and you can arm-knit a couple of the other blankets if you wish. If you haven't arm-knitted before then I suggest you practice with some spare yarn, or even some string, until you can make the stitches evenly. Due to the scale of the knitting, it's clearest to show the method using photographs.

CASTING ON

This long-tail method requires you to estimate how much yarn will be needed before you start casting on; you'll need approximately 1–2 forearm lengths per ten stitches to be cast on.

1 Unwind the required length of yarn from the ball.

2 With the length of yarn (the yarn tail) unwound from the ball, make a loop by taking the working yarn (the yarn coming from the ball) over the yarn tail. Reach through the loop to take hold of the working yarn and draw it through, hold this section firmly while pulling gently on both yarn ends to tighten the slip knot.

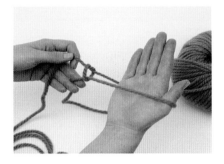

3 Slide the slip knot over your right hand and onto your wrist, adjusting the yarn to make the loop sit snugly on your wrist. The two ends of the yarn will be hanging from your wrist, arrange them so that the yarn tail sits to the left-hand side and the working yarn sits to the right-hand side.

4 Pass the yarn tail over the palm of your left hand, looping it over your thumb. The yarn tail will be the lower section of this loop and will lie closer to your wrist.

5 Pass your right hand under the lower loop on your palm and over the upper loop.

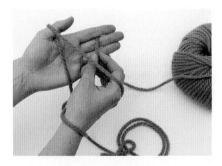

6 Take hold of the working yarn and draw your hand back through the loop over your left palm.

7 This new loop will become the stitch. Once it has passed over the loop on your palm, slide it over your right hand and onto your wrist.

8 Draw the stitch to sit fairly snugly on your wrist by pulling on the yarn tail and the working yarn in turn.

9 Repeat these steps to create the required number of stitches, sliding the previous ones up your arm to make space.

KNITTING THE FIRST ROW

The stitches are knitted with the working yarn, the end attached to the ball. To avoid confusion, fold and knot the yarn tail left from casting on.

1 With your right hand pick up the working yarn from underneath, so that the yarn passes between your thumb and first finger, and hold it securely in your right fist. Use your left hand to pick up the first stitch on your right arm.

2 Lift the stitch, pass it over your right hand, and drop it. The yarn held in your right hand will be drawn through to become the new stitch.

3 The new stitch needs to be rotated slightly before being placed onto your left arm, so the section of the stitch that lies over the front of your arm will lead directly back to the ball of yarn. This prevents the stitches looking twisted on the finished piece.

4 Adjust the stitch by pulling on the working yarn so that it sits snugly on your wrist. Repeat these steps to knit the remaining stitches from your right arm over to your left arm.

KNITTING THE SECOND ROW

This row is worked exactly the same as the first row, the only difference being the direction in which you are knitting and passing the stitches. You will now be picking up the stitches from your left arm, and knitting them onto your right arm.

1 Begin by picking up the working yarn and passing it under your left thumb, so that it lies in the palm of your left hand, and hold it securely in your fist.

2 With your right hand, pick up the first stitch and bring it over your left hand, drawing the working yarn through the stitch as you do so.

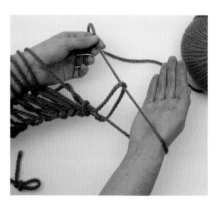

3 Insert your right hand into the front of the stitch, rotating the stitch so that the working yarn lies across the front of your arm, and slide it onto your right wrist. Ease the working yarn to secure the stitch snugly to your wrist.

4 Repeat to knit the remaining stitches on your left arm in the same manner. Following rows will follow the same instructions as for first and second rows, depending on whether you are knitting from the right arm to the left, or the left arm to the right. This will create stockinette (stocking) stitch.

BINDING (CASTING) OFF

Once you have knitted the required amount of rows, you will need to secure the stitches by binding (casting) off.

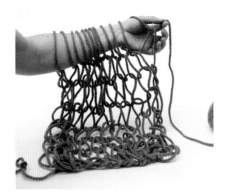

1 Finish a row with the stitches on your left arm and knit the first stitch onto your right arm.

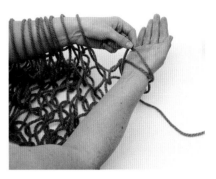

2 Repeat to knit the second stitch in the same way. Use your left hand to pick up and lift the first stitch on your right arm over the second stitch, bringing it over your right hand and dropping it.

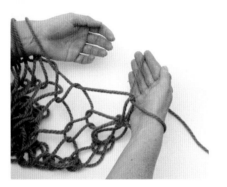

3 Knit the next stitch from your left arm onto your right, and repeat the process of passing the first stitch over the second on your right arm. Continue working across the row in this way.

4 Once you have worked across the row there will be one remaining stitch on your right arm. Loosen off the stitch slightly before sliding it off your arm. Feed the working yarn through the stitch and gently pull it up tight to fasten off the final stitch.

Suppliers

I used my own yarns and giant needles for several of the projects in this book, and can ship worldwide, but if you prefer to buy closer to home, look for yarns advertised as "giant," "jumbo," or "extra bulky," made from pure wool. You can also use the Yarnsub website, www.yarnsub.com, to find suggestions for substitute yarns.

The following list includes other suppliers I used for particular projects.

YARNS

Lauren Aston Designs
USA: www.etsy.com/shop/laurenastondesigns
UK: www.laurenastondesigns.com

Cascade Yarns
USA: www.cascadeyarns.com
UK: www.lovecrafts.com

Rowan Yarns
Stockists on website: www.knitrowan.com

Melanie Porter
www.melanieporter.co.uk

OTHER MATERIALS

Pom-pom makers
USA: www.amazon.com
UK: www.amazon.co.uk

Felt (slippers)
Ncfelt Supplies
www.etsy.com/shop/ncfeltsupplies

Non-slip (slippers)
Sock Stop from Rico Design
www.lovecrafts.com

Hot water bottle
Fashy 2.0l
USA: www.amazon.com
UK: www.amazon.co.uk

Polystyrene beans (bean bag)
Wilson and Grimes
www.wilsonandgrimes.com

Silk ribbon (keyrings & hanging decorations)
Habotai Silk Natural Dyed Ribbon
from Lancaster & Cornish
www.lancasterandcornish.com

Tassels (tassel cushion)
ColourfulBeadshop (Violet Earth Supplies)
www.etsy.com/shop/violetearthsupplies

For general craft supplies:

USA

JOANN Fabric and Craft Stores
www.joann.com

Michaels
www.michaels.com

UK

John Lewis
www.johnlewis.com

Hobbycraft
www.hobbycraft.co.uk

Index

Acknowledgments

I owe so many "thank-yous" to people who have helped me with this book, both in the long-term and short-term. To my parents, Adrian and Alison, frankly for getting me here in the first place, and my husband, Alex, for supporting and encouraging me every step of the way. To our dog, Harry, for entertaining me and hassling me to get out the house, and to my friends Leanne and Sally for their constant help and dependable support.

Huge thanks to Cindy Richards, Penny Craig, Sally Powell, and the rest of the CICO Books team, first for commissioning this book and giving me such a wonderful opportunity, and then for their steadfast belief and continuous support (which can't have been easy at times!). Great thanks and admiration to Kate Haxell for wading through my waffle and somehow making it legible and "proper." Thanks to Penny Wincer and Joanna Thornhill for the beautiful photography and styling, and Marilyn Wilson for testing patterns and working out what was going on!

Lastly, I'd like to thank my dear friend Jayne for unknowingly reminding me to keep things in perspective and for tirelessly demonstrating how to tackle any problem with dignity, grace, and when appropriate, a bottle of gin.